Serviced Accommodation Success

Leverage and Monetise the Hottest Trend in Property Investing

Kevin Poneskis

GW00535743

Serviced Accommodation Success by Kevin Poneskis
www.sasbook.co.uk

Design by Luke Bunting
Research by Kevin Poneskis
© Copyright 2020 Kevin Poneskis

Note for Librarians: A cataloguing record for this book is available from Library and Archives Canada at www.collectionscanada.gc.ca/a-z-index/index-e.html

Printed in Peterborough, Cambridgeshire, UK ISBN: 978-1-909846-63-0

Published by Progressive Publishing
Progressive House
Units 8, 9 & 10
Cygnet Park, Forder Way, Hampton Peterborough, PE7 8GX

www.propertysoldier.co.uk
Email: kevin@propertysoldier.co.uk
Facebook: Property Soldier Kevin Poneskis
Instagram: propertysoldier
LinkedIn: Kevin Poneskis Property Soldier
YouTube: Kevin Poneskis Property Soldier
Twitter: @PropertySoldier

Proofread by Matthew Armstrong of MA Services
Email: fao.armstrong@gmail.com

READ THIS

Hi there, firstly a big thank you for purchasing your copy of Serviced Accommodation Success.

I hope that this book will give you the information you need to make a huge success from property investing, just like I have been able to.

I have crammed as much knowledge and expert advice into this book as I can BUT the world of serviced accommodation moves fast and I constantly have more I want to share with you.

That's why I have created a bonus online resource for you. This online resource will help keep you up-to-date with the latest changes and give you a competitive advantage over other property investors.

To get immediate access to your bonus gift - go here now before you continue reading:

🔍 | WWW.SASBOOK.CO.UK

Kevin Poneskis

About the Author

Kevin Poneskis has been investing in property since 1991 when he was a 20-year-old soldier in the British Army. Kevin served for 24 Years and retired at the Rank of Regimental Sergeant Major serving most of his career in a Commando Regiment. He left the Army aged 40 without the need to get a job because of the ongoing income generated from investment property. Kevin left the army in 2011 with 11 single lets or Buy to Lets (BTLs) and a House in Multiple Occupation (HMO). He has gone on to grow a multi-million-pound property portfolio, adding to the BTLs and HMOs with Serviced Accommodation (SA) properties, but has also bought, refurbished and sold many properties along the way. At the time of writing Kevin, with his Fiancée and Business Partner Caroline, has either bought, or bought and sold over 50 properties.

In more recent years Kevin discovered SA and decided to focus on SA as his main income generating property strategy. This book will explain why Kevin chooses SA over HMO and BTL and why you should seriously consider this strategy too.

Kevin has been featured in the best-selling book *Property Trend Setters*, which is a testament to the fact that he is right on trend when it comes to property investing! He also produces a podcast called *the Serviced Accommodation Property Podcast* which regularly ranks in the top ten in the world for business downloads.

Acknowledgements from the Author

This book has not been easy for me to write. It has taken me a year and a half to complete and only with significant help from my fiancée Caroline have I made it to the finish line! I would also like to thank all the people who have contributed their stories and experiences in support of my desire to provide a comprehensive and accurate reflection of the Serviced Accommodation (SA) business model and how it can be used to change lives for the better.

Introduction from the Author

24 years in the Army taught me the importance of self-discipline, teamwork, learning and implementing systems and last but not least, that we should all lead by example. I know that if a soldier wants to be successful and climb up the ranks, he or she needs to embrace and excel in these four areas.

In my property investing career I soon found that I could employ a lot of what I had learnt as a soldier to achieve success in property investing. Of all the different property strategies I have tried over the years, SA has produced the greatest results for me by far in terms of cash flow and the time it takes to get it. I decided to create a step by step SA system that is easy for me and my team to follow in order to build, optimise and run an SA business. The system I have created and explained in this book is called the DEALS system, which you can also use to give yourself the best chance of cashing in on this exciting and relatively new strategy.

Once I achieved a senior rank in the Army, as all leaders do, I sometimes had the very difficult responsibility of asking people to do things that might actually put them in harm's way, and in doing my duty I would put myself in harm's way too. Now as a civilian, life is so much easier because I now only ask people to do things that are in their best interest! I am a firm believer in leading by example and I think we should all practice what we preach and guess what, I now do what's in my best interest too! If someone asks my advice on how best to make good money fast in property without the need for significant seed capital, my answer now is to learn about SA!

This book is intended to help people who are either doing or are interested in doing SA. Many things in this book are correct to the best of my knowledge at the time of writing but may change in the future. Please visit *www.propertysoldier.co.uk* for details of my upcoming training events in order to stay up to date with all the latest information surrounding SA.

My Property Investing Education

One of the reasons I am now a successful property investor is because I have been on many property education courses. Since 2010, when I started paying for property education, I have spent in excess of £100,000 on training and mentorship. Two of my main mentors right now are Mark Homer and Rob Moore from Progressive Property. I am very grateful indeed to the people who have taken my money over the years in return for teaching me how to make as much money as possible from property.

The standard of training from the many different training companies I have used has ranged from just ok to outstanding and looking back, some of the training was pretty expensive for what I got, but on reflection, you just have to make the best decision you can at the time when deciding whether to pay for a training course or not. Sometimes there were sales techniques used by the person selling the training and both the good and bad training companies use similar techniques which draws criticism from many. When the training delivered is poor then the criticism is fully justified, but the problem is that the good training companies get tarred with the same brush as the bad. The fact is that if I personally had not been sold to by someone and convinced to pay good money for training, I would probably still be in the Army, or if not in the Army, then still in a job in which I would not have created the level of financial security that I currently enjoy.

I now also deliver property education and guess what? People pay to attend my courses and I am very proud of the fact that I have helped many people transform their lives financially and I get a huge amount of satisfaction from that. Some people are criticised because apparently "they've only been doing property two minutes and now they're teaching it"! I think that if someone is relatively new to property it's not necessarily wrong for them to start teaching as long as they don't attempt to mislead people by exaggerating their experience and what they are qualified to teach. I left the Army in 2011 having been a property investor for 20 years. I left without the need to get a job because of the income I was generating from property. A little over a year after I left the Army, I started teaching people to do what I have done which is to create wealth from property.

I am a firm believer in leading by example and I would never ask someone to do something in property unless I have either done it myself or am currently doing it, and only if I firmly believe it is in their best interest. I have turned down people's money on multiple occasions when I didn't think it was right for them to pursue certain property education and training. When it comes to the training I provide, I know I am giving good value for money as the information and support I give people can be life changing. I have invited some of the people who have attended my SA training to tell their story and explain how this training has helped them progress as Serviced Accommodation operators. I am very proud of what people say about my courses and the results that many people go on to achieve. I am sorry if you are reading this and you know that your story could have been featured, but I have to strike a balance and not have too many.

CONTENTS

Section 4: Acquisition 113

Section 5: Logistics 195

Section 6: Scrutinise 243

SECTION 1: INTRODUCTION

#01. What is Serviced Accommodation?

Serviced Accommodation is a term that's used to describe very different things by different people. Even property professionals and professional bodies use the term differently. It can be used to describe anything from a room in an owner/occupier house that is let to guest on a short-term basis, right through to large hotels. Anywhere you can lay your head where there are services provided could be deemed to be Serviced Accommodation.

Many of the people who do my training will embark on the strategy that I like to call 'whole house' or 'whole apartment' SA. This is for a guest, or group of guests who all arrive at the property on the same day and leave on the same day and as the name suggests take the whole property for exclusive occupation for a period of time. The property is provided fully furnished and kitted out as a home from home which provides an alternative to a hotel for short or long stays. It is cleaned in between guests and returned to show home condition. Bedding and towels are provided and usually toiletries, tea and coffee. This may be with a single unit (house or apartment), or whole blocks of apartments or a new build development. For tax purposes, the business may fall under the Furnished Holiday Let criteria, or the Serviced Accommodation criteria depending on which services are being offered.

For simplicity, throughout this book I will use the overarching term of Serviced Accommodation (SA), unless there is a need for me to be specific.

#02. Why Serviced Accommodation?

Serviced Accommodation is the most 'On-Trend' property strategy right now and there has never been a better time to get involved. I have been investing in property since 1991 with Buy to Let, Houses in Multiple Occupation and buying and selling/flipping property, but I can honestly say that I am no longer as interested in those investment strategies. When a tenant leaves one of my properties now, I either sell it or I convert it to SA. At the time of writing I recently sold two properties that I decided would not work as SA and I am currently selling another three. I literally DO NOT want any more tenants! Last year I was forced to evict TWO sets of tenants through the courts. I had to evict them because they were not paying me rent and were also trashing my properties. I get so angry just thinking about this. I can get my head around the fact that tenants will sometimes stop paying rent for a multitude of reasons, but when they also deliberately damage the property at the same time, that's just impossible to reconcile for me. Please don't misunderstand me here, over the years I have had many good tenants, but unfortunately if you do BTL or HMO for long enough you are going to get some bad ones, and when you do it's a game changer that's for sure!

Many BTL landlords are happy with £100- £200 cash flow per month from their properties, and many are simply happy to break even and rely on capital growth and this can go on for several years which unfortunately can lull you into a false sense of security until you get that bad tenant who might have been good for years but then turned bad. When you factor in the number of months it takes you to get them out of your property and the legal costs involved and the cost of putting the property back into good condition again, from my experience £10,000 is not an unrealistic figure that you will have to swallow in terms of lost income and expenditure. How many years of cash flow will this wipe out? I know people will say that you can pursue people through the court to recover the money, but that is not a bed of roses either.

I recently evicted a tenant who cost me an awful lot of money, and I later discovered that he had moved back to Poland and so I decided not to try to pursue it further. The other decision we all have to make when it comes down to pursuing people through the courts is how distracting this is and the amount of headspace this takes up. This can be extremely detrimental to your life in general. It can affect you family life and your health, and it is also likely to take up time that you could be putting to good use on other things. Instead of finding your next property deal that could make you tens of thousands, you are chasing someone for let's say £5,000. You are risking wasting your time and getting nothing or very little back from the courts. I do agree that you should at least try to get a County Court Judgement (CCJ) on the tenant so that they cannot easily inflict themselves on another unsuspecting landlord, but please don't turn the whole thing into a vendetta because it can harm you in the ways I have just mentioned. On another occasion the Magistrate neglected to mark on his paperwork that I wanted to pursue the tenant being evicted for all of the unpaid rent and so I was told that I would need to start the whole process again. I decided that this was not in my best interest and I decided to move on with my life.

Before I learnt about SA, I thought that the odd 'bad apple' tenant was just one of the things that you had to put up with if you wanted to create recurring or residual income from property. SA has shown me that I can not only get recurring income, but I can significantly increase that income. Yes, you can have the odd misbehaving SA guest, but the power that a guest has over your property and your life is tiny compared to that of a tenant. I will cover what steps are necessary to protect yourself from bad SA guests, and with these measures in place we find that bad or troublesome guests are rare.

I used to be under the impression that SA was fancy property that was mainly apartments in the posh parts of town. I now know differently. Yes, SA does work really well in the nicer parts of town with the nicer properties, but it also works really well in the more modest types of property not in the 'poshest' of areas. I know this because I now have many ex BTL properties that are in terraced streets around the country, that are in what would be considered a cheap place to buy. The original reason for buying property there was because the BTL yield was good, that is, the purchase price versus the rental income was good. I have now discovered that the very same properties work really well as SA too, but the yield has now increased by about 500%. That's 500% of the BTL income and assumes that there isn't going to be a bad tenant that wipes out five years of the BTL profit! I know people may say that you could also get a bad SA guest, but my experience is that if you set up and operate your SA business correctly, you are so much less likely to have this happen to you, and besides, even if you did, you will have been enjoying much more income from the property as SA in the interim period. People will also mention that you can insure against damage and loss of rent, but I found that the vast majority of BTL tenants would not pass the qualifying criteria for an insurer to cover, and if they did pass, they are extremely unlikely to cause you a problem and so you may well be spending out a lot on insurance unnecessarily.

One of the main plus points for me of having SA guests instead of tenants is that your guests do not have tenant rights because it is not their 'Principal Private Residence'. They actually live somewhere else. A guest cannot claim the right to stay in a property without paying as they can in rental property. In my expert opinion and experience, if you do SA correctly, then a guest should not stay without having already paid in full. Should they wish to stay longer, or their stay is unauthorised, you have their credit card details to settle the bill. If you need to, you can also fall back on a damage deposit from the guest, taken before their stay begins. These simple steps help to ensure that the guest pays for their stay, and if there is some damage to the property or contents, on most occasions, you can settle the issues within the life of the stay or soon after. Best of all, no court and greater peace of mind!

Why is SA Such a Great Opportunity Right Now?

E-commerce or internet shopping is a major reason because people are now comfortable searching for what they want to buy online, and when they find it, they are happy to pay for it via the internet and now most SA booking and transactions happen this way. People search for their temporary accommodation online and more and more are choosing SA. More often than not people provide their credit card details and depending on the payment terms, pay immediately or at a later date but always prior to check in.

Smartphones make running an SA business so much easier because we can do most things these days on a smartphone which can free us up from a desk or office making it a truly 'mobile' lifestyle if you'll pardon the pun. Smartphones make it so much easier for people to book our SAs too. Someone could be at home or out and about and using their phone easily to search *Booking.com*, find an SA property and literally by pressing the screen a few times, book and pay.

High Speed Internet and the fact that over half the world's population are online makes it so much easier these days for us to run an SA business and for people to find us and book our accommodation.

OTAs (Online Travel Agents) - well known trusted brands like *Airbnb, Booking.com* and *Trip Advisor*, who spend hundreds of millions of dollars on their marketing annually. Despite the fact that these companies are spending such vast amounts of money to drive customers to their websites, they allow us to advertise our SAs on their sites for free. They will charge us a fee when someone books, which is typically around 15% of the total booking cost but we only have to pay them if we get a booking, which is a great business model for an SA business owner. As an example, if you get a booking of £100 you would then need to pay the OTA about £15. I think that's a really good deal! The really great thing to consider here is that you are only required to pay commission to the OTAs for the initial introduction to that customer. Once a guest stays with you, there is no rule that stops you inviting them to book with you directly next time via your own website, or simply by calling you. You can offer them a discount which would be easy for you to offer because you are not paying an OTA commission. We typically offer an 8% discount on a direct booking.

Why Does SA Work So Well?

The quick answer is there is high demand for short stay accommodation in towns, cities and holiday destinations. If you take a two-bedroom apartment or house for instance, you could easily sleep five people in there. You can have two in each bedroom either on single beds or both in a double and you can have a sofa bed in the lounge that sleeps at least one person. Some people opt for zip and link beds that are large single beds that can be made into a king. I will cover this option in a later section because there are pros and cons to zip and link. Five people who need short stay accommodation could easily represent three hotel rooms. If your accommodation is listed on *Booking.com* (the largest short stay accommodation provider in the world), your unit will appear in the search results for five people alongside the hotels. To keep the maths simple, let's say that these five people want to stay in your town or city for five nights and a hotel room is £100 per night. In the hotel it would cost these five people collectively £1,500 whereas they could stay in your two-bed apartment for let's say £1,000, saving a massive £500 on their stay.

That's the first reason they are likely to choose the SA over the hotel. The second reason is they will be seeing that they are going to be getting the whole property to themselves in the price (I will cover SA properties where a guest only can book a single room in a house in a later chapter). They will see in the photos that they are getting a lounge to themselves as well as the kitchen along with whatever else the SA has to offer, which could be a garden or other outside space. The property is set up as a 'home from home', usually with a fully equipped kitchen, Wi-Fi, toiletries, bedding, towels etc.

The feedback I get from people who have young children is that they much prefer SA over hotels, because they feel their children are less likely to disturb other people because of the sometimes 'wafer thin' walls of some hotels. Sometimes parents prefer to have their kids in a separate bedroom to their own and so SA can provide a perfect solution for that and in some cases, can even save the guest money during their stay.

I have found that tradesmen and tradeswomen (I will just call them trades) are looking more and more to stay in SAs over hotels. In the past trades would look for a hotel to stay in first and an SA second, but that behaviour is shifting more and more towards SA first and hotel second. The reason I hear most often is that if they stay in a hotel, they end up spending too much money at the hotel bar and restaurant. In SA they are less likely to drink in the evenings, and if they do, they might simply get some cans of beer in, or go out and find a cheaper bar or pub to drink in. Along with buying drinks at the bar people also buy their evening meals and breakfast at the hotel. When people stay in an SA, they will often visit a supermarket on the way and get their food and drink for the duration of their stay and end up eating healthier food and save money at the same time!

Many trades have a set budget per night for their accommodation and typically this budget will only stretch to the cheapest B&B or guest house. More often than not the trades have to supplement their allotted accommodation budget to cover the total cost of a hotel or guest house. This is where the cheaper houses in the less posh parts of town really come in to their own because often the combined daily accommodation budget is enough to cover the overall nightly rate of the SA property. For instance, if the five tradesmen have £25 per night each, that's £125 per night that they have to spend collectively, and they are likely to choose a two or three bed SA property that sleeps five if they are fortunate enough to find one! You might have a two-bedroom terraced house that ordinarily would let out for £600 per calendar month and you could get £625 for a five night booking! Often you will get bookings of several weeks and even months, which for a full month you could get £3,875 at full occupancy.

If you select your location correctly and have a track record of providing quality SA, then it's possible to get immediate results from a 'Goldmine Area'. For example, I was completing the dressing of a new SA property when I had a one month booking on the two-bed flat of £3,500, and I received the booking before I had even paid the first month rent. Yes, you did read that correctly. I rented the property from a landlord in order to do SA and paid market rent for it of £600. This is called Rent to SA (R2SA) which I will be covering in a later chapter. With that property I was able to get a month-long booking from a large local company without even having any inside photos of the property to show. This was because the company knew, having used my service before, that the SA accommodation I provide is at a high standard and they were happy to book on faith knowing the guest would get a comfortable peaceful stay.

People also choose SA over hotels as they are less likely to be disturbed by the neighbours. Most of us will have been in a hotel and the passers-by in the corridor have woken us up late at night or early in the morning, and sometimes people in the next room can be making far too much noise! Yes, I know what you're thinking but it could also be a crying baby, an argument or a party. In an SA you also get a nice sofa or chair to watch TV, or to read a book, whereas often in a hotel there isn't a sofa or armchair to use, and the list goes on.

Throughout the book, I will be sharing with you some examples of people who have discovered SA, who I have had the privilege to train and/or mentor, whose lives have been changed by pursuing this strategy. Many are now good friends of mine and some are getting involved in giving back and training others to get the same success as they are enjoying. Dan is one such example, he has implemented many of the acquisition strategies described in this book and here is his story so far:

Dan & Vicky Eaton –
Pivotal Serviced Apartments

❝ In August 2017 a friend suggested I attend a property event; he had recently been to one and had been greatly inspired by what he had heard. I had left the Royal Navy about 5 years previously to enjoy more time with my young family and had moved to the corporate environment. Although a successful move from a career perspective, it had become stale and in reality, I spent a lot of time away from the family with long hours each day and little flexibility around work patterns. What was worse was that the future only seemed to hold much of the same. Although I didn't appreciate it fully at the time, I was in the perfect frame of mind for a property event. The weekend I spent at the event listening to Kevin Poneskis describe property strategies and a way of approaching life and work that was a polar opposite to my corporate experience was a pivotal moment in my life and I remain truly grateful to my friend for the recommendation. It opened my eyes to possibilities I hadn't even realised were available. My inner entrepreneur was dancing with excitement.

Shortly after returning from the property event, whilst processing what I had learned and researching properties and areas locally, I was pointed towards a landlord who, due to a change in market dynamics locally, found himself with a block of eight apartments and only four of them rented. A sophisticated property investor, this landlord was open minded, and after some lengthy discussions, was willing to try something different. We agreed that I would take on two of the vacant apartments and turn them into Serviced Accommodation with a management agreement in place to provide guaranteed rent to the landlord. My wife and I set up our first property company – Pivotal Point Properties trading as Cheltenham Serviced Apartments - and began to get the two apartments ready for guest bookings. It was fairly straight forward physically preparing the apartments; setting up a channel manager, payment processor and accounts with booking platforms was more challenging. It took two weeks of hard work from reaching the agreement with the landlord to being open for bookings. Unexpectedly, during that two weeks, the landlord reached out and offered that it would suit him better if 'we would just take over the whole building with the current tenants in situ'! With some trepidation, but with a mounting anticipation of the possibilities, we agreed and became landlord to four sets of tenants and a provider of Serviced Accommodation with four apartments to offer. At that time a friend was in a tricky personal situation and needed somewhere to live and it was a lovely feeling being able to help by offering a practical solution and we rented him one of the four apartments at very reasonable rates; this also helped us as it allowed us to phase the preparation of that apartment.

It was a steep learning curve, and as I sat in the classroom, having already booked myself onto Kevin and Caroline's Serviced Accommodation course, I was very reassured by having access to the expertise and experience that was available.

Over the next few months, the guest bookings started to build up and our experience developed concurrently. Each problem encountered was tackled and the solution built into a process. An operations manual evolved - I'd like to be able to say that in accordance with best practice, and following the course teachings, that this was completed before the first guest arrived, however our reality was something quite different and somehow it kept slipping down the list. 'What to do when....' questions were addressed as they arose - such as 'what to do when a guest calls late in the evening in

December to advise that the storage heaters had been turned off and have no heat and the apartment is freezing'.... Answer – don't tell the guest there will be heat tomorrow, but get out the *Dyson* heater from home, de-ice the car, take it to the apartment, apologise to guests and add 'replace storage heaters for electric radiators' to the top of the to-do list. There were many moments of advising guests 'we'll get back to you' whilst hastily re-reading the course notes and working out a solution. With the benefit of hindsight, I view all these problems positively as a test of our processes and an enabler to the development of a resilient system.

By the end of the first six months we had also taken on two further Rent to SA properties that had appeared on the local rental market and opened those for guests. With both letting agents there was absolute transparency about the use of the apartments; we wanted to be sure that any reputation we gained was for the right reasons. Opening up new apartments had become much easier; there was already a team in place locally – housekeeping, linen, reliable trades for maintenance; we now knew exactly what needed to be put into the apartment, where to source it and had business accounts set up with those suppliers; and with the systems already in place for managing bookings and payments, adding on a new property was now a task that took hours, rather than days.

It was at this time we bought in admin support in the form of a Virtual Assistant to help with the increasing guest communications. It was a low number of hours to begin with and there was of course a period of training, but once they were up and running, the support was very welcome and allowed us more time to focus on developing the business and not getting lost in the day to day details.

The summer of 2018 was a very busy time. Each time one of the block's tenanted apartments was vacated, we undertook a refurbishment program and turned it into Serviced Accommodation; between June and September three more of the eight apartments transitioned to the guest portfolio and the last two were completed during the Winter and so by the start of 2019 we had ten guest apartments fully operational. During the 2018 summer I was approached to manage two apartments locally that had already been set up for SA but were in need of new management. From the outset our SA strategy was to develop experience and credibility as a Rent to SA operator and then to utilise that to scale the business through management of other people's SA. This opportunity therefore fitted neatly with the strategy and so the management stream of the business began. Through attending network events, another contact was made who had an apartment to manage, and so by the first anniversary of the company the portfolio had thirteen properties operating; had generated significant monthly cash flow and a first year turnover of £245k.

Soon after, again through networking contacts, we were approached by a group of investors who had a block of apartments in Greater London that were in dire need of new management; the block of twelve apartments had been recently converted to accommodation and the developer had worked with an SA management company to find investors for the apartments with the intention that the SA management company would then operate them on their behalf. Unfortunately, the SA management company quite quickly became unable to continue and the investors were left, almost overnight, with the burden of the apartment costs and no guests. We put together a rescue deal, working alongside the developer and the investors, and took on managing nine of the twelve apartments (the investor of the other three apartments was already an SA operator and decided to manage the three themselves). The apartments were already prepared for guests, had a housekeeping team ready and so as quickly as we could get the apartments marketed, we were ready to go, and they started being booked.

Clearly 'Cheltenham Serviced Apartments' wasn't going to work as a trading name. As speed was of the essence to get the apartments operating as quickly as possible, we had to register a second trading name and began operating. Once we had them running, we had time to more thoroughly consider the company name. At the outset, the initial properties were all in

Cheltenham and so the name made a lot of sense – easy to be found, says exactly what it is and easy for guests to remember. Now with two locations, consistency difficulties arose – simple things like, what do you say when you answer the phone (you don't know which location the caller is calling about), two sets of logos and templates, making sure guest communications refer to the correct trading name. It was obvious that this was clumsy and needed streamlining. So, we registered yet another trading name – but this time, one that could be used in perpetuity – "Pivotal Serviced Apartments". This fitted nicely under the umbrella of Pivotal Point Properties and also within the Pivotal Point Group that had been put in place to encompass Pivotal Point Properties, Pivotal Consulting, and also Pivotal Homes – the Developments arm of our growing property businesses.

It was in July 2019 that I was able to leave my full-time corporate job and begin operating under Pivotal Consulting with time to focus on both SA, the Developments and perhaps most importantly, the family.

Concurrent to the development of the SA business, we were introduced via networking to a contact who had two SA units they wanted managing. As part of building a relationship and getting to know our client, it transpired they were predominantly inclined towards developing property. Over a period of about a year we looked at potentially converting commercial property into residential to run as SA; after a number of false starts with various opportunities coming and going, we eventually ended up taking on a part finished building site. This came to my business partner via networking from a contact that, co-incidentally, we had helped set up their own SA unit some months earlier. Not wanting to cover the reasons for it being up for sale here, suffice to say, it was a series of tragic circumstances. The project was more new build than conversion, but we pulled together a team to take over the site and we were then officially developers!

From there, we purchased a dilapidated shop and attained planning permission to convert it into five flats that will be used as SA. Around the same time, again through a contact met networking – an opportunity presented itself to purchase an old GP surgery that had planning permission to convert to five flats and build an additional seven in its car park. We negotiated, offered and eventually agreed to purchase the building using a combination of Investment and development finance. This, like the shop is now an ongoing project. Some of the units will be sold, some will be rented out and some will be utilised for SA - a 'convert to SA' model. We now plan to scale, replicating this model and at the time of writing, have just had an offer accepted on another building which will be converted to twelve flats.

And where are we going next? From that first property event and Kevin and Caroline's course, to where we are now has been challenging and hard work, but exciting. We have learned a lot in these two years, both as a business and as individuals. With tested systems and processes, with the key organisational enablers of admin support and call management embedded, with practice at taking on and setting up groups of units, we can now take on, or convert, blocks of apartments and assimilate them quickly and effectively into our portfolio. We are now positioned to scale. We are ready to seize the next opportunity. And the one after that. 🙶

#03. Introducing the **DEALS** System

D ue Diligence

E xplore

A quisition

L ogistics

S crutinise

If you want to create and run a business, you have to create a logical easy to follow system for you and your team to follow. If you want to teach others how to create and run their own similar business, the system must be memorable and flow in chronological order. The system must allow for continuous optimisation and improvement, which is a must for any business to reach maturity. The system I have created is called the DEALS system which provides the 'End to End' steps, as well as the ongoing work to do which is vital to achieve ongoing success.

SECTION 2: DUE DILIGENCE

#04. Where Should You Choose to do SA - Where is Your SA 'Goldmine Area'?

This a question I get asked a lot. There are many factors to consider and lots of boxes to tick but it's simply a case of meeting as many of the criteria (which I will cover shortly) as possible and not over analysing it. One of the most important factors in my opinion is finding an area where there is a demand for SA which is as close to where you live as possible. I call these SA demand points. In my opinion most towns and cities will be fine to do SA in, it's simply a matter of finding a good spot in that town or city. The reason that I recommend doing SA in a town or city as near to where you live as possible is that most people in the early stages of their SA business will be heavily involved in the set-up of each of the properties as well as meeting with cleaners. If you choose a location that is too far away, you are going to be spending far too much time travelling. Yes, it is possible to outsource all of the onboarding work of an SA and if you are super confident that you have the person or people in place to do this for you then yes it is ok to pick an area that isn't close by. However, please be aware that circumstances change, and relationships change, so don't make the decision to choose an area far away from you lightly.

Once you have a tried and tested team in place for your SA business it is ok to move away, and to let the team do all of the physical work like meet and greet, maintenance and acquiring new units. My fiancée and business partner Caroline and I have a full team in place in South Wales which is where we lived when we set up our SA business, but now we live in Lincolnshire. We are no longer required to be in any of our SA locations for our business to function and grow and we are able to oversee and manage the business remotely using a phone, phone Apps and a laptop.

When choosing your SA Goldmine Area, you should always focus on demand for SA. One of the helpful indicators of demand is whether there is a hotel relatively close by. If there is, then the hotel will have done a lot of legwork for you. Remember I wrote earlier about why people will choose to stay in an SA rather than a hotel, and the main reasons are saving money, extra facilities and privacy. So, if people are going on to *Booking.com* to look for somewhere to stay in your town or city and they find a hotel in that area, they will also find your SA unit if you're listed on *Booking.com*. When there isn't a hotel in a certain area, it doesn't necessarily mean that there isn't a short stay demand, it might just mean that despite the fact that there is demand a hotel just hasn't been built there yet! Where there is no hotel, you simply need to be assessing the demand yourself and I will list some examples of this demand. This is not an exhaustive list as there are many things that will cause people to go and stay in a different town or city for a while and so you just have to use your own judgement on a specific thing you spot in an area that might create demand. What you are looking for is all year-round demand to maintain profitability in the winter to supplement the typically high summer months. Here are some examples:

Near to a Train or Bus Station

People may want to stay near a bus or train station if they intend to commute from your location to another. It may be that the cost of accommodation is significantly cheaper where you are which makes the commute financially worthwhile. This is certainly the case in places like London where accommodation can be very expensive. It is worth mentioning here that the need to provide a parking space for travellers arriving by train or bus is less, although your guests might hire a car on arrival. It's likely that the main train or bus station in a city is going to be in the city centre where it can be the case that parking is very limited and many hotels and SAs do not offer parking there.

Construction or Building Sites

Many of the trades/builders/contractors working on site will not live locally and so they will need temporary accommodation in hotels, guest houses and SAs. Remember that you can be extremely appealing to groups of these contractors for the reasons mentioned earlier. When it comes to parking you need to remember that often the vehicles that they drive are high sided so check the headroom of your allocated parking space if you have one and make it very clear to your guests via your listing on the OTAs and your website when they book. Construction sites like this can provide year-round demand if it is a large project.

Industry

This could be something like a power plant or a steel works, or a large port which will have a natural 'rhythm' of work which will require larger amounts of specific trades at different points in the year. Travelling trades will need a place to stay.

Big Business

Large businesses, companies and organisations often have mobile workforces to supply skilled staff to construction, industry or directly to customers' homes. Big business is an opportunity for repeat custom as they may visit the area repeatedly for annual services for example.

Town Centre

The centre of a large urban area will represent a cross section of differing demands which might include construction, industry, big business, holidaying or a combination of all of them. People visiting could therefore be for both work and leisure purposes.

Airport

Yes, there is going to be good all year demand, but please be mindful of the fact that you are likely to attract mostly one-night stays from people travelling on flights and this will significantly increase your costs. The main costs involved in an SA business are the cleaning and laundry. It's much more profitable for you when your guests book for longer because for up to a seven night booking you still only have to pay for one clean and change of linen. When near to an airport I would encourage you to reach out to the airport staff and the airlines that operate out of that airport and offer your SA as an alternative to hotels. One of the main complaints of aircrew is that they are always living out of a suitcase and they never have a base to be able to leave things in between flights. I know of lots of people who have SAs near airports who are block booked by groups of air crew or by an Airline on behalf of their flight attendants. You can offer a significant discount on your nightly rate in order to secure a nice long booking and in the process make a lot more money than you would from multiple frequent short stays, which also come with a higher admin burden.

Sporting Venues

As well as the obvious reasons people will visit, these places are also used by artists and bands. A nearby SA to a sporting ground can also be booked long term by the respective club to provide a better and perhaps more cost-effective solution to hotels for visitors to the club. Many sporting venues also have conference centres that will attract people from out of town too.

Golf Clubs

The more prestigious the better. As well as the reasons given for 'Sporting Venues', groups of golfers are likely to book an SA for a week when on a golfing trip or break. If it is a championship course, then you can expect to earn serious money when the course hosts a tournament. Please just be aware that I wouldn't choose an area for SA if it only had a golf course as the main attraction. I would be looking to tick other boxes as well, because golf as well as many other sports can be very seasonal, with demand in the summer and not so much in the winter.

Conference Centres

The busier the better, the larger the better. The conference centre is extremely likely to have hotels located nearby and for the reasons given earlier you can provide a better alternative for your guests.

Tourist Attractions

These can be national parks or areas of natural beauty, historical sites as well as theme parks to give just a few examples.

Hospitals

Clearly there are going to be lots of scenarios where people are going to be admitted into hospital for long periods of time, and often a relative or family will want to be nearby to make visiting more convenient. The other scenario to consider is the people working in the hospital for long periods of time. We had a consultant who was working in the local hospital book one of our one bed apartments for just over five months whilst on assignment.

Universities

These are a regular source of bookings. There will be multiple open days and graduations that will cause families to travel in order to see their loved ones graduate and be in the photo that ends up on the mantelpiece for ever.

The list above is not an exhaustive; each area is going to have its own unique reasons for people wanting to go there for short stays. It's just a case of finding as many of these as you possibly can before making a decision. If you are straddled between two areas, then I suggest you just do your research and make a list of the different SA demand points in each location and choose the one with the most! The other thing that might sway your decision here is if a particular location has people there who would be willing to help you if required, because we all need a little help from time to time!

Another thing that will help you find the SA demand points is to *Google* your town/city and then click on the *Wikipedia* option. Here you will find lots of information about your area, and if you're like me you will find out lots of information that you previously knew nothing about. Often people live in an area their whole life and they know less about it than a visiting tourist finds out on one visit. By doing some research you will discover some SA demand points that you might have overlooked otherwise.

#05. Who is Your Target Market?

Once you have established your SA demand points you will know the type of people who are likely to be using your SAs. The three main categories are white collar workers, blue collar workers and leisure guests. This will help you decide on the type of property that would be suitable for your guests, in what area, and how to present it. One of the main considerations is the sleeping arrangements. If you are targeting the trades, then you might decide to provide single beds in the rooms instead of a double or king/queen size bed. This will clearly be more appealing to groups. Trades are less likely to have an issue sharing a room as long as they have their own bed. Even with single beds you will still get booking from couples, who ordinarily would prefer a double bed, but ultimately this preference is not as high a priority as convenience or saving money.

The white-collar workers who are at the executive end of the pay scale are going to expect a more expensive property in a 'nicer' part of town and the blue-collar worker (the trades) are going to be happier with a more modest property in a less 'exclusive' area. Most people looking to start an SA business will overlook a street or area if it has terraced houses, but the average house price there is low and the average rent is low too. We will look at this in more detail later when I cover R2SA, but my rule of thumb is if you feel safe there and you are happy to leave your car outside then your guests are likely to feel the same way.

It is worth mentioning that guests staying for holiday/leisure purposes, or not there for work reasons, will stay in both high end and moderate properties. There is no point trying to second guess these guests and try to cater for them. All you can do is attempt to cater for your most likely guest type depending on the demand research and then welcome whoever arrives! When people book, they will see that you are offering the property as SA in a certain location with the facilities listed and photos of all the rooms provided and if they decide to book at the advertised price then so be it. I will cover photos of your property in a later section but it's worth mentioning that you should always show the photo of what the property looks like on the outside on your listing as well so that your guests know exactly what they are booking because often a place can look stunning from the inside photos but from the outside it might be a regular terraced house.

Paul Selman – Anchor Accommodation

" When I started in property a little over a year ago, I didn't know where to begin, never mind what SA was. After starting to attend property events my eyes were opened to the possibilities and I noticed an opportunity present itself for Serviced Accommodation after speaking to a local construction firm near me. So, I booked on to Kevin's course as I knew there was a deal to be had but didn't know how to structure it properly. The information delivered and knowledge I gained on the SA Intensive and the 6-month Mastermind I joined was fantastic and really made the difference when it came to structuring the company I eventually started.

After running the analysis on my local area, it soon became apparent that R2SA might be a little tight, so I approached the construction company again and simply asked where they needed accommodation. They had contracts all over the UK and were spending a fortune on hotels. On the first deal I was able to source a four-bed property 15 minutes from their work site at a fraction of what they were paying the hotels. The contractors were staying in a much more comfortable environment and I was making a profit of £2640 pcm from one unit. So, Anchor Accommodation was born. I now offer similar services to other companies where I am able to source and furnish accommodation to fit their unique criteria at a fraction of the cost of hotels and provide a much superior quality of life for contractors for stays of 3 months plus.

The profits that I have earned have allowed me to re-invest into other operators SA units, as well as start a property sourcing and development company, B-Hive Property, with my business partner Ben in Manchester. The community and the specific courses and mastermind programmes have changed my business and personal life immeasurably and I am so glad I made the commitment I did a year ago. Thank you to Kevin and his team for all their knowledge, guidance and support...I can't thank you enough. 🙶

#06. What Type of Property Works as SA?

This ranges from a basic studio apartment to a penthouse in a fancy waterside apartment block. From a one-bedroom house, to a large mansion. You simply match the property to your most likely guest type and as with any business you should always cater to demand if you want to make the most money!

#07. What is the Correct Planning Use Class for SA?

There is a lot of confusion about the correct use class for SA, because there isn't a specific use class that fits all types of Serviced Accommodation units. In the UK Class C (C1 - C4) covers Hostels, Hotels and Dwelling Houses and 'Sui Generis' is a classification which falls outside of typical C1-C4. I have referenced the UK 'Planning Portal' in order to explain this:

C1 "Regular hotels" (+ guest houses / B&B).

Certain SAs may fall into this category if they are letting out by the room to guests who are not in the same party or group. In the case where people in the house are checking in and checking out on different days, as opposed to a large group all arriving and leaving together as part of the same booking, the use of the property is clearly more like a hotel.

C2 "Residential hospitals, schools, nursing homes".

Clearly not the correct use class for SA

C3 "Dwelling house as a principal or secondary residence".

You can see that it states here that C3 is for dwelling houses including secondary residence, so if you own or operate a C3 property as SA, letting it out on a short term basis, there is no need to change the use class as long as you are not letting it out by the room and there is no other material change of use. I like to call this 'whole house' SA.

C4 "Houses in multiple occupation (HMO)

Small shared houses occupied by between three and six unrelated individuals, as their only or main residence, who share basic amenities such as a kitchen or bathroom"

I do not intend to cover HMO's in great detail because this is a book about SA, my intention is only to make the distinction from a planning point of view between SA use of a property and HMO use of a property.

A lot of people get confused because they think that it is ok to do SA by the room in an HMO because it is already letting out by the room, but the main distinction is that an HMO is the occupants' only or main residence. An SA guest will not be occupying the room as their only or main residence.

Something to consider is that if you are regularly accommodating overseas guests for prolonged periods of several months on a by the room basis, under these circumstances, it may be deemed that the property is in fact their main residence and may now be considered to be C4 HMO. As well as the planning C4 use class there are strict rules and regulations with HMOs regarding licensing and health and safety.

To be clear, a C3 property used as SA on a whole house basis, is not an HMO because it is not anyone's "only or main residence".

Sui Generis (a Latin phrase that means "of its/his/her/their own kind, in a class by itself," therefore "unique")

If the way a property is used is too far outside one of the recognised classes, then 'Sui Generis' might be the use class decided by the local planning authority for that property. If an SA operator wanted to use a property for HMO tenants as well as SA guests, he/she could ask for Sui Generis. I would advise against operating SA in this way because I think you are likely to have complaints from HMO tenants and SA guests alike, unless your property allows for good separation between guests and tenants, and you would probably need a change of use to Sui Generis to have the proper permission in place to be allowed to do it. The other scenario where Sui Generis might be appropriate is if you have a larger house which is C3 and you are regularly letting it to more than six guests on a whole house basis.

The Planning Portal defines Sui Generis as "Certain uses do not fall within any use class and are considered 'Sui Generis'. Such uses include, betting offices/shops, payday loan shops, theatres, larger houses in multiple occupation, Hostels providing no significant element of care, scrap yards, petrol filling stations and shops selling and/or displaying motor vehicles, retail warehouse clubs, nightclubs, launderettes, taxi businesses and casinos". Notice it says 'such uses include' so they are leaving room to be able to apply Sui Generis to anything that isn't properly identified elsewhere.

Change of Use Class

It may be necessary to apply for a change of use when a 'material change of use' has occurred in a property. Usually a change from one use class to another involves a planning application to the local planning authority and it will decide whether or not to grant planning permission. The local authority may become aware that a property is being used in a certain way and may feel that the current use class for the property is not appropriate. If this happens you may be asked to stop or reduce that particular activity or apply for change of use to the appropriate use class.

What Constitutes a Material Change of Use?

In SA this scenario is most likely to be from C3 to C1/Sui Generis when there are significant changes to the following:

Parking

Many people assume that because a property starts to be used for SA that the parking demand will increase but this is not necessarily the case. Most SAs in the UK operate between 70-80% occupancy so therefore 20-30% of the time there is no parking requirement. Often your guests will arrive having walked from a bus or train station, or they arrive by taxi, and it's quite rare that guests arrive in more than one car and so you can see that an increase in parking demand is not usually the case. If you make it clear to your guests on your listing and after they have booked what any parking restrictions/limitations are, then there should not be a problem regarding parking. People are very accustomed now to finding the nearest car park or finding the nearest on street parking space and walking back to the SA. The thing to remember is that if the property was being used as a family home, then a normal household today often has more than one car and the property is occupied 95-100% of the time.

Patterns of Arrival and Departure

There is no reason why your guests should come and go from the property any differently than tenants or homeowners and remember that there is no one using the property 20-30% of the time. If there was a normal household using the property, the occupants might be working irregular shifts and that could be a lot more disruptive for the neighbours.

Number of People

In my opinion this is going to be the main issue that is most likely to cause neighbours to complain, but as long as you have some control measures in place you should not have too many people in your SA property. The number of people you allow to book will depend on the size of the property, and the number of bedrooms and bathrooms. I would recommend that you only advertise for a maximum of five people if there is only one bathroom. A two-bedroom property could sleep six at a push if the bedrooms are big enough for two, there is room for a double size sofa bed and there are at least two bathrooms. If you cram too many people into a property you are likely to get bad reviews which will cost you financially, so it's really not worth doing it. Conversely, even if you have a property that can sleep five or six, your average number of guests will probably be below that, and you will be empty 20-30% of the time. Even with a two-bed property, when booked you will often only have one person in each bedroom, but remember to charge an extra 'person per night' rate on an SA for the additional occupancy. More on extra person per night rates later.

'Over occupancy' is when guests under state the number of guests staying at the SA at the point of booking to avoid additional person per night charges. The impact on the business is additional cleaning and laundry, some wear and tear, but mainly a loss of income. To deter over occupancy, some SA operators inform their guests that for their safety there are external cameras at the property. Some people have a camera facing outwards on the front door (if there was a back door you would need the same) that is motion activated and can record the comings and goings at the property. If you have a large property which only gets booked by a small number of people you can restrict access to a bedroom that isn't needed using an internal lock or combination lock, which will reduce the cleaning and laundry requirement. If it is clear to someone booking that you are likely to be monitoring the number of people staying, then they are unlikely to risk being asked to leave the property and not get a refund because they broke the terms and conditions of the booking. Having said all this, in my experience people trying to over occupy is rare and remember a normal household may have a large number of people living at a property so it's worth putting this issue in to its proper context.

Frequency of Party Type Activity

This is something that gets highlighted in the press because people love to read about a mass *Airbnb* party. A party at our properties is a rare occurrence, probably because we have some measures in place as a deterrent. We make it very clear in our terms and conditions that parties are not allowed and if ever there is a booking from say a group of young women or men that makes a party scenario more likely we reinforce and highlight the rules and make it clear that we will be notified by neighbours of a party and if this happens they will be asked to leave. If you take a deposit in case of damages, it also makes a party less likely. If your property is close by to the night life in your town you should seriously consider putting a two or even three night minimum booking limitation on the property. We have two night minimum stays across all of our properties in order to reduce the likelihood of a party and also because the cleaning and laundry costs make one night stays a lot less profitable. Most people who are looking to have a party in an SA will look for a property that allows a one-night stay first and will not want to pay a deposit and they won't want to see strict terms and conditions relating to parties. Remember most of your guests who don't intend having a party will not mind this, in fact they will welcome it. We occasionally have people cancel their bookings when they read our terms and conditions and we are very happy when this happens for all of the reasons mentioned above. When someone does cancel their booking, it frees you up for someone else to book who is happy with your terms and conditions.

Refuse and Recycling

A little common sense and some proper monitoring and controls will prevent any issues occurring. There is no reason why your guests should create more rubbish than a regular household, but the fact is that a regular household is much more able and willing to adhere to the local rules regarding recycling and rubbish collection days and routines. If your property is in an apartment block, then there is less likely to be an issue because there is usually a communal bin area and your cleaners can simply put the rubbish there when they clean, and the bin collection will happen as normal. An SA house needs much more attention because more often than not the residents in the street or area put the bins out at particular times and days and often the local recycling rules need to be adhered to otherwise the bin men won't collect the rubbish. Sometimes your cleaners will be prepared to take the rubbish away as part of the cleaning cost, but make sure you make this clear when you get your cleaning quote, otherwise they will be reluctant to cover this extra task for the same money. When the council provide 'wheelie bins' you can ask your guests or cleaners to place the rubbish in those. If there are no bins and residents put black bags out the night before a collection or in the morning, we provide a large external plastic bin. I recommend that you get one that has the lid attached otherwise it will blow away in the wind when not secured properly. If the guests are staying for more than a couple of days they are likely to want to place rubbish outside to prevent a smell build up from food or perhaps nappy waste and if there is a bin outside this can be done with no need to worry about attracting animals including birds that will tear open the bags to get at food. As you can imagine if the rubbish management isn't properly dealt with, it could easily lead to complaints from neighbours to the local council, but with a little forethought and planning you will be able to avoid that.

So you can see that with a properly run SA there is no need for a material change of use to take place, and if someone from your local planning authority suggests to you that there is, you should ask for the evidence or justification to support that. It might be that a particular neighbour is making regular complaints, but you could easily show using your channel manager and cleaning schedule (these topics covered in a later section) exactly how many people have stayed and when and if there genuinely isn't an increase or problem with the categories listed you will be able to prove it.

90-Day Rule in London

'The Greater London Council (General Powers) Act 1973' stated that "all short stays less than 90 days are deemed material change of use and therefore subject to planning". In 2015 the 'Deregulation Act' stated that "short stays up to 90 days per year are not subject to planning". As you can see, the rules were relaxed in 2015 meaning that short stays can take place in London for up to 90 days per calendar year. Many people ask me "how do you get around the 90-day rule in London"? My reply is always you shouldn't try to get around the 90-day rule, but more importantly you don't have to in order to make really good money doing SA in London. Some people decide to do SA in London for four to five months of the year in which time they can cash in on the 90 days of short stays allowed, and then let the property out on an AST to a tenant for the remainder of the year. The main point I have to make here is that stays over 90 days don't count toward the restricted 90 days, so if you get a booking of over 90 days that booking will not take away your allowance of short stays.

At the time of writing *Airbnb* is the only OTA that is counting down the number of bookable nights in a calendar year that are available and it is not coordinating with any other OTAs or with SA operators on bookings received from other sources, which means that you as the SA operator will need to keep the running total because no one else, including the local authority will have this information. A point to note is that if you get a longer than 90 day booking via Airbnb, they will not deduct from your 90 short stay allowance. The 90-day rule makes it even more important to go and source longer bookings. You can approach local businesses and companies offering them a discounted price that reflects the fact that you will have much less cleaning, laundry and maybe meet and greet cost, as well as no OTA commission to pay. If your long-term rate is good you can also get a longer than 90 day booking from Silver Door or Situ (covered later), or other similar companies in the market. So, a little more effort than just relying on bookings from the OTAs can make you a lot more money with no need to breach the 90-day rule.

The Map below shows the outer boundary of the 32 London Boroughs that are affected by the 90-day rule. Many people believe that it is everything inside the M25 but as you can see this is not the case.

#08. Who Are Your Competitors?

I recommend that you closely follow and scrutinise your competition. By this I mean take a look at hotels and other SAs in your area, go and stay there! You will be able to see what is being done well and what is being done badly and model your SAs accordingly. I suggest that you look at *Airbnb* and *Booking.com* listings in order to do this and aim to replicate the ones that get 4.5 or above stars out of 5 on guest review scores on *Airbnb* (*Airbnb* review scores from guests tend to be higher than *Booking. com*) and above 8.5 out of 10 on *Booking.com*. You should be mindful that some operators will have fake reviews. They invite friends and family to book their units probably at a discounted rate (because *Booking.com* and *Airbnb* charge a percentage of each booking) and leave a really positive review and score. This can sometimes be easily spotted because you will see that the genuine reviews leave a poor score and criticism of the SA and interspersed are really positive ones. When this manipulation hasn't taken place, it is more likely for you to see a regular pattern and not so many polar opposite reviews.

When you are looking at the good listings with good average reviews, what is it that the guests are reporting positively on? This might be a nice coffee making machine, or a nice table and chairs outside or convenient parking for example. Whatever is working well, look to replicate and maybe enhance to be even better than the competition. A useful tool you can use on *Airbnb* is to look at the forward bookings that a particular unit has got. When a listing accepts 'Instant book' you are able to see this. You should take into consideration how many bookings this listing is getting at that price point and what reviews they are getting at that price. Some *Airbnb* operators are not necessarily running a tight business and they might not have the optimal price point so only aim to replicate what they are doing right if they are also getting good bookings. It's worth mentioning here that often when you hit the sweet spot on your listing, you will get a lot of bookings within a few weeks of check in. This is because many travellers for whatever reason are last minute bookers and when they go on to *Booking.com* all of the cheap SAs are taken and therefore don't even show up on their search. If you're not too cheap you will still be available to be booked at this time and you will make a lot more money per annum if you get this balance right.

#09. Managing Your Pricing

It's all about testing and tweaking your rates. You also have to bear in mind that rates can be seasonal so please don't set and forget. You should refine your prices, or have someone else regularly doing this for you, to optimise your income. If you find an *Airbnb* listing that accepts instant book you should check that it is also on *Booking.com* at least because if it isn't then there is no point in taking any notice of its forward bookings because if it was also on *Booking.com* it is extremely likely that it would have a lot more bookings. Many *Airbnb* operators do not know that they can also list on *Booking.com* and make a lot more money!

Depending on the size of your property, you should set a minimum night rate. This is especially important with a larger property that sleeps lots of people. For example, if you have a three-bedroom house that could sleep seven people, you might set a minimum price that reflects a four person booking. Let's say that your minimum nightly rate for this house is £200. Even if one person wanted to book and stay, the price would still show as £200. In this situation it is unlikely this person will book because they are likely to see hotels at a much cheaper rate and probably one or two-bedroom SAs at a much cheaper rate. That said if this individual still chooses to book, then who are you to argue. What you don't want to happen is you allow that person to stay for only say £100 per night, and because that person booked you didn't get a booking from a party of four who would have happily paid £200 per night if they had seen your listing and been able to book!

You also need to decide on your 'extra person per night rate'. This is the rate that you charge per person over and above your minimum rate, which in our example would be the same whether one person books or four. So, let's say that your extra person rate is £25 per night then if you got a booking for seven people then the total price charged per night would be £275. Again, if you had been booked by the sole person at £100 you might also have missed this booking. The effect is compounded because people will often book for much longer than one night and so this can have a significant financial implication. On all of our SAs, we do not allow one-night stays. I will cover how to deter people from booking whose intention is to have a party later in the book, but the financial incentive for having a minimum two night (or more) booking rule, is to significantly reduce costs by reducing your cleaning and laundry costs, incentivising longer bookings, which will make you more money!

#10. Understanding Your Costs

Now that you have studied the competition and you have a good idea on how much you can charge per night you need to work out your operating costs. For this you need to get quotes. The main costs to find out for your individual properties are:

- Insurance

- Furniture and soft furnishings

- Cleaning & Linen / Laundry

- Meet & Greet

- Utilities Inc Broadband

- TV License

- Council Tax / Business Rates

Insurance

I recommend that you seek the advice of a specialist broker to ensure that you have the right level of insurance for your SA business. You will need insurance for your operating company and property specific insurance so get quotes for both.

Furniture and Soft Furnishings

Depending on your own situation, you can either buy furniture for your SA or hire it. Get quotes on both and decide if capital outlay is more important to you or cash flow in order to make your decision.

Cleaning and Housekeeping

I strongly recommend that you don't entertain doing the cleaning yourself on your SAs. Ok, you might in the very early days do the odd one yourself, I can honestly say that I never have, but I know that some people do when they are starting out. There is plenty of money to be made from SA and the cleaning of them should definitely be paid for out of the turnover if you want to be able to scale and avoid becoming overwhelmed. The cleaning is undoubtedly one of the most important parts of your SA business to get right as it will be one of your main overheads and it's important not to be paying too much per clean as this will have a significant compounding effect over time.

As well as deciding if you will be able to work with your cleaners for a long time and grow with them, you also need to get accurate quotes from them. It might sound a little obvious, but this is a vital part of the process, because there are so many variables and before getting into a business relationship with anyone both sides need to be very clear on what they expect from the other. My advice is that you ask what their hourly rate for cleaning is and please bear in mind VAT. Does their price include VAT? If they are not yet VAT registered then ask if they are likely to become VAT registered any time soon, because when they do, they will probably need to pass the costs on to you. Most people will start their SA business with a new Ltd Co. which doesn't have any existing turnover and therefore it will not need be VAT registered to start with. I will cover the VAT implications of running an SA business in more detail in a later section. Once your turnover has hit the requisite threshold, which the government change periodically (visit *https://www.gov.uk/vat-registration-thresholds* to get the current rate) you will need to be VAT registered and when you are, you will be able to claim back the VAT element of your cleaning bill, so as you can see, it's important to consider and plan the VAT implications when choosing your cleaners.

Now just because you have established the hourly rate, and let's say that it's £12 +VAT, it doesn't mean that it's going to cost you £12+VAT to have your small one bedroom flat cleaned. It's important to ask the cleaner how many hours they will charge you for a clean. Yes, it might only take them an hour to clean a small one bed flat if it hasn't been left too messy by the previous guest, but would they really be willing to do it? The reality is that they will often need to drive across town to get to your flat and carry the new laundry up the stairs (if there isn't a lift) as well as their cleaning equipment, do the clean and then carry everything back down to the car - would it really be worth it for them to do all that for £12? If you manage to get a cleaner to do it for that price you will have done very well, or at least initially, because I would guess that they initially agreed to do it, but after a while they will tell you they need to up their price or they will start to look for an alternative contract that is less work or more money and it might be too late to re-negotiate once they tell you they are quitting. The majority of cleaning companies will have a two hour minimum charge. The key point I am trying to make here is find good cleaners and pay them a fair price if you want to keep them. If you have more than one property you need to confirm what the price will be for each property. The price will go up the larger the property is and relative to the number of bedrooms, and if you do have more than one I recommend that you get the cleaner to visit the property with you before confirming the price, otherwise there may be an issue further down the line if the cleaner says that they didn't realise the property was so large or it was so hard to get to, etc. when they initially quoted.

You also need to establish from the outset what you want the cleaners to do for you when they quote. Your cleaner will usually be the first person to visit your property after your guests have gone and there are some really important things that need to be done at this time. I will go into detail around the role of your Housekeeping team in a later chapter.

Linen and Laundry

As with furniture you can hire or buy, and you should use plain white hotel standard (you add colour by using cushions and throws). Commercial laundry companies may offer to source linen for you to buy at a discount from their suppliers, especially if you are going to use them on a regular basis to launder your linen. Others will offer a hiring service which includes laundry which is good for cashflow as you won't be buying the linen. It might be the case when you are first starting out that hiring linen is not a viable option because there will be a minimum weekly cost and it might be too expensive for you to use them until you are able to give them more laundry to clean due to economies of scale. Depending on the quotes you receive you can decide whether to hire or buy.

The amount of linen required for an SA is often underestimated and I advise that you take advice from the laundry company/linen hire company on this. If you are going to buy your own, my advice is that you need three sets of bedding per bed, which allows for one on the bed, one in the wash and one on the shelf. You should have this set of three for each 'turn' you are likely to do in a week, so if you are likely to have three turns in a week, you should have nine sets of bedding per bed. So if you have a three bed house and you average three turns in a week (say three, two night bookings) you will need 27 sets of bedding, and this will depend on your clean linen being dropped off weekly, because if it is longer between drop offs, you will need more! If you hire your linen, then this won't be a problem because the linen company should ensure that they have the right level of stock themselves.

Meet and Greet (M&G)

I am a big fan of Meet and Greet and I will point to the benefits of it many times in this book. If an SA business wants to scale, then the M&G will need to be outsourced and so the cost needs to be factored in from the outset. Some housekeeping companies also offer this service so get quotes from them if they offer a one stop shop.

Utilities and Broadband

It is down to you to pay these costs, not your guests. The easiest way to work out how much this will cost is to look at your own bills at home and estimate. If you don't live in a typical house in the UK, then you can ask someone who does. Another useful resource is websites like *Zoopla* where estate agents and letting agents advertise property to sell or rent; at the time of writing *Zoopla* has a tool that will give you the estimated running costs of the property.

The average occupancy of an SA in the UK is between 70 - 80% and so on some bills, like electricity, your bills will be lower. You should bear in mind that many apartments don't have gas, but rely on electricity instead, which will clearly eliminate a gas bill but increase the cost of electricity. The TV licence is simply a case of entering 'UK TV Licence' into your browser and you will get the current rate. If you have multiple properties in a block you may qualify for a hotel TV license which will bring significant savings over a TV license for each apartment. When it comes to broadband, some suppliers will insist you go on to a commercial tariff if you put the contract in a company name. These will sometimes be more expensive than a residential tariff, but the service may be more personal to you.

Council Tax

At the time of writing there is also a Council Tax Calculator Smartphone App available which is useful. I wish all letting agents and estate agents knew about this app as none of them ever seem to know how much the council tax is on a property when asked, and they always say they will get back to you and let you know - don't hold your breath for that one!

Will the Property you are Analysing Make Money as SA?

A rule of thumb is that after working out your costs, your SA should be able to break even at 50% occupancy at its minimum rate i.e. with one or two people booking for one night at a time. You will be able to estimate what your nightly rate will be by analysing the other SAs in the area. If there are not enough comparable SAs in your area, ensure there is demand (covered earlier) and find similar property in a similar town or city nearby to arrive at what your own nightly rate will be. People who attend my training get access to my Deal Analysis System, which helps them understand night rates, competitors, costs etc., and more importantly training on how to use the system to determine what the potential profit is on each property being analysed. People also use the analysis system when working with joint venture partners to help with raising funds structuring deals.

Company Set Up and Accounting

How much will your accountant charge you for doing your accounts. You can set up your Limited Company (Ltd Co.), or companies at minimal cost yourself. At the time of writing you could do it yourself via the Companies House website (UK) for £15. There are other online sites that are more user friendly that you can use for a small fee in the region of £30, or you can ask your accountant to do it for you and typically they will charge you £100 - £150.

I would recommend that you do use an accountant to do your accounts and to give you advice on the financial and tax implications of your business. There are lots of moving parts to an SA business and in my opinion, you should be looking to outsource as many things as you can from the outset, because if you don't you will end up juggling far too many things. If done correctly, there is lots of money to be made in SA and therefore you could and should use some of the income to pay for others to take on as much of the work as possible. If you do this, you will be able to scale/grow your SA business. If you don't you are likely to experience overwhelm and limit the size of your business which will in turn limit your income generating potential.

I would also recommend that you appoint an accountant who has a high level of experience of SA. Please do not take their word for it that they know what they are talking about. In my experience the vast majority of accountants are not knowledgeable enough when it comes to SA to be able to advise you correctly. If you already have an accountant or need to appoint an accountant, I would ask them if they have any clients on their books that have an SA business and if they don't, I think you should seek another accountant with more knowledge and experience. Otherwise you will become a guinea pig for them to learn the business, and you will ultimately pay for any mistakes made. Paying for these mistakes could simply be in the form of you paying too much tax on your business because your accountant interprets the HMRC rules in a certain way due to a lack of experience. I give the details of my accountants to people who attend my training courses. I do it this way because otherwise they would be swamped with enquiries and initial free consultations.

This book will be read for many years to come and so I would like to keep the content as 'evergreen' as possible and my accountant, or 'power team member' may or will change over time. After reading this book you will be able to ask your accountant some specific questions and if the answers given differ significantly to what's written in this book then you will have a decision to make. I will cover my recommended company structure for your SA business in a later section.

Marketing

Spending money on marketing your SA business should be a serious consideration. If you rely solely on the OTAs for your bookings, you could be missing out on a lot of potential revenue from long term bookings from companies and businesses.

I do not want to give too much specific advice here, as where your marketing spend is directed will be guided by your marketing strategy and marketing plan, but any marketeer will tell you that the way to market any business is a very fast changing 'picture' and is specific to the business situation. Therefore, any specific advice on marketing given here will soon become out of date. So, make sure that you budget for some marketing spend. I cannot tell you how much because that depends!

Systems

Please see the systems section later in the book. The type of business you have will dictate the systems you will need in place to help and support you and these will need to be budgeted for. The main system you will need to budget for is your channel manager which at the time of writing can range in base cost from £20 per month to £120 per month depending on functionality and robustness.

Staff

Please see the team section that comes later. The type of business you have will dictate the team members you need. These team members could be anything from a handyman to a personal assistant (PA). Your team should grow in conjunction with the size of your business and the cost of the team should be budgeted for.

Dave and Leanne Gooch – Jurassic Coast Property

" I first met Kevin at a property training event and being a military man myself his reasons why he got into property really resonated with me. I immediately signed up for my wife and I (Leanne was 4 months pregnant at the time) for the SA Intensive course. We are based in Poole and believed this was the perfect place to set up our SA business and begin our property journey to becoming financially free. These 2 days were the perfect introduction and provided us with the step by step blueprint of how to set up, maintain and systemise an SA business.

As a natural progression we continued our learning by joining Kevin and Caroline on the 6-month Mastermind mentorship (with Leanne obviously having to take a break halfway through to give birth to our second child). Firstly, to use the wealth of knowledge that all the mentors have to propel us in the right direction and secondly the chance to be held accountable, to remain focused and motivated to succeed. Not only did the mastermind sessions guide us through making that first phone call to an agent, to that amazing moment when you are handed the keys to your first SA unit but it also opens you up to a whole nationwide community at every stage.

We couldn't have set up our successful company Jurassic Coast Property LTD and expand our family without the help, guidance and support of Kevin, Caroline and their wonderful team! We are excited about where our SA journey will lead us next...

SECTION 3: <u>EXPLORE</u>
Setting Up Your Business

#11. Terms and Conditions

I strongly advise that you ask your guests to sign your terms and conditions before they are allowed to stay and preferably as soon as they book. We occasionally have people cancel a booking when they read our terms and conditions which we are more than happy with, because who knows what their intentions may have been otherwise! You are able to specify in your listings that terms and conditions will apply, which enables you to get support from the various OTAs if for any reason a guest resists signing your contract.

Your terms and conditions should include as a minimum any activity that you do not want to take place in your property. For example, smoking and parties, which are the most common things you will want to avoid. You should clearly state what charge will be applied if evidence of smoking is found by the housekeepers and what exactly will happen if you find out there is a party going on. Will the guests be asked to leave with no refund as they have breached your rules? You should also be clear on check in and check out times and that no business use of the property is permitted.

Payment Policy

You will need to decide how and when people pay you. More often than not people pay using a credit card, but sometimes we allow a bank transfer. If you allow a bank transfer, you should also ask for credit card details in case of damages. Some SA operators ask for the money for the booking to be paid at the time of booking and at the other end of the spectrum some take payment at check in. We choose not to ask for the money at the point of booking because many people will book you months in advance and the majority of people don't want to pay so far away from their stay. Most people want to have the flexibility to allow for a change of plans and so if your terms and conditions required payment at the time of booking, most guests are likely to book with someone else instead because there are still likely to be other options available to them so far from check in.

We choose to take payment two weeks from check in which seems to be perfectly acceptable to our guests. Occasionally when we attempt to take the payment at this point the card is declined, sometimes this is because the card has expired, but more often it's because there aren't enough funds on the card to pay for the booking. One of our team will contact the guest to notify them that the card has been declined (via whichever OTA the booking came through) and to arrange an alternative payment card, or to allow for extra funds to be added to the existing card. Sometimes you will be unable to contact the guest because they don't reply to their email or phone. In this case, you will need to decide how long you give the guest to update their details before cancelling the booking, as you want to give yourself enough time to get a booking in for the same period. We find that quite a lot of bookings come in within two weeks of check in, so this isn't too much of a problem if you have to find an alternative booking, as long as you act quickly.

The reason we don't allow people to pay when they arrive at the property is because they might not show up and if at that point you try to charge the card you may find that the card is invalid or doesn't have enough remaining credit on it. Another reason is that on the day it might be the case that the card is declined for whatever reason and the guest is struggling to pay. You will then find yourself in a situation where the guest may want to pay you in cash which I would advise against allowing as that is a tactic used by people who are involved in criminal activity. Criminals don't want to give credit card details and they might not be intending to treat your property very well and that's why they don't want you to have their valid card details. They also don't want their payments to be traceable through the banks if they are running a largely cash based business. Alternatively, the guest might ask to stay initially with the promise that payment will be forthcoming, and you don't want to be in that situation because payment might never arrive. The guest might be having genuine financial difficulties, or it could be a regularly used tactic by this person who preys on naive and inexperienced SA operators with the aim of staying for as long as possible, before leaving without having paid. Please don't be too alarmed here, the vast majority of people who book are honest law-abiding citizens, but there is no reason to be vulnerable to those who are not.

Refund Policy

Our policy is that we don't offer a refund once payment has been taken. As per our payment policy this means that two weeks from check in there is no refund. Outside of two weeks from check in we have not taken any money and so there is no money to refund if a guest cancels a booking. If you choose to take payment on booking, you will need to decide on what your refund policy is going to be. If the payment is non-refundable a long way in advance, you may find you don't get many advance bookings. A downside to having payment taken up front with a fairly flexible refund policy, is that there needs to be an admin process every time someone cancels a booking to see if they are within their allowable refund period, then refund whatever has been paid if they indeed are. As far as possible, you should try to automate your business, especially if you intend to expand to a large number of SAs.

Deposits

Deposits can be taken, either by actual payment or by pre-authorising an amount on a card, mainly in order to cover the cost of potential damages. Sometimes you will be unable to charge a credit card if there are not enough funds on it. Some areas in the UK are more likely than others for SA operators to require a deposit, with London being the most likely place. In an ideal world, every SA operator in every location would be able to take a deposit and still get plenty of bookings. The reality is that in most areas of the UK, SA operators don't take deposits because very few other SAs in the area are asking for a deposit. This means that if you are the only SA asking for a deposit, you will struggle for bookings because people will naturally go with the SA which doesn't require a deposit over the one that does. Even if the guest has no intention of causing damage, the reality of the matter is that accidents do happen. Even though the guest may have no intention of avoiding paying for something if they damage it, the fact is that you are holding their deposit. They do not know that you will be honest or fair with their deposit, nor how much you will take from it in order to repair or replace an item. Often you just need to take a pragmatic view, if it's only a small amount of damage, is it really worth the hassle of asking the guest to pay and potentially disagreeing over whether they caused the damage or not. A bad review should be avoided if at all possible and a well-run SA should make plenty of money, so we often choose to treat minor damage as a running cost and absorb it.

Minimum Age Restriction

You are allowed as per your terms and conditions to impose a minimum age for your guests, but you should ensure you are not breaking any laws based on where you are operating. Some SA operators do not allow children, because children can be the cause of damage whether it be knocking things over or drawing on walls. You might even have a minimum age restriction on your lead guest who is the person booking and usually paying, and you could also have an age restriction on all of the guests who stay, for instance you might not want an 18 year old to book with three 16 year old friends.

Parties

In my opinion, you should have a 'no parties rule' unless you have a detached property nowhere near other houses and you choose to run a specific party venue, taking into account all the pitfalls. Parties are the most likely reason for you to get complaints from the neighbours and is the most likely thing to cause damage. If you don't make it very clear people may claim ignorance. We make it clear that if there is a party, we will ask the guest to leave the property immediately and there will be no refund. This might be the time that the booking is cancelled which is fine by us. If you have an SA that is close to the nightlife in town, it might be wise to have a two or even three-night minimum stay to make a party less likely, as people are usually going to book the place that allows a one night stay first.

Parking

If you can always offer parking for your guests you are going to be in greater demand and you will be able to charge a higher night rate, but if you can't offer parking it's not a showstopper. When you are doing your due diligence on your competitors (existing SA units) you simply need to see how many are offering parking. If there are lots that do, you will have to accept that you are probably not going to be able to charge the same nightly rate as they can. Many hotels and SA units in the city centre inform their guests that they will need to park in the nearby public 'pay as you go' car park, or even find on street parking which is normal these days. It is possible for you to pay for parking permits for car parks and on street car parks, and this might be a good solution for you to provide this for your guest as you would be able to get a discount for a bulk buy or renting a specific parking space for a long period. Be aware that you will need to check whether the permit is pre-printed and requires a specific car registration which clearly won't work. You also need to be mindful of the fact that if you have a permit that doesn't require a registration, it will not take long for one of your guests to inadvertently drive off with it which will cause you the hassle of getting it back and having one ready for your next guest!

Minimum Night Stays

As mentioned earlier, one-night stays make it more likely that you attract a guest who wants to have a party, but it also means that you proportionally have more costs from cleaning, laundry and meet and greet deducted from your single booking income. So, in a nutshell, setting a minimum booking period of two or three nights equals a longer stay, more profit due to a lower proportion of costs to income and less chance of parties.

Pets

A significant consideration is whether you will allow pets in your properties. My advice is that you only allow pets in a house, but you will also need to be mindful that if you are offering outside space, which you probably should, then the garden or outside space should be secure enough to prevent an easy escape. A mentee of mine recently decided that he would stop allowing pets to stay in his property due to the fact that a dog had drowned in the nearby canal. He determined that it would be far too expensive to build a good enough fence to be able to prevent pets from getting out and he didn't want to be dealing with distraught pet owners complaining to him that he hadn't provided a safe place for their pets to roam.

I think in most cases it's best that you don't allow pets in an apartment block because you don't know how big or loud or dirty the pet may be, and some leases don't allow pets for residents. So, houses are going to be better and I would suggest a detached house to be even better for noise reasons. If you are going to allow pets, you should charge a higher night rate or cleaning rate for pets and also take a deposit (or higher than normal deposit) to reflect the likelihood that there will be more cleaning required to remove pet hair and potentially pet smell. Pet owners are likely to accept these extra costs because the alternative is often to leave pets with long suffering friends and family or pay significant sums to kennel their pets. Many pet owners do not like to leave their pets, and often the pets don't like to be left, so an SA that allows pets is going to be in high demand and your price can reflect this.

Check In/Check Out Time

A typical time for your guests to check in or check out by is 2pm - 4pm and 10am - 11am respectively. Although this can be any time you like but remember too late a check in time or too early a check out time will deter some guests from booking. The main consideration for you is that there needs to be enough time for your cleaners to get the property cleaned and ready for your next guests to check in if you have back to back bookings. Remember that you might not be the cleaner's only client and so they may have several other cleans to do that day so a decent four to five-hour window during the day for the cleaning is recommended. Once you've got several units in an area serviced by the same cleaners, from time to time, you are going to have multiple cleans taking place on the same day, so your cleaners will need enough time, especially if there aren't many cleaners on their team.

Early or Late Check In or Check Out Fees

If your guests would like to check in early, it is normal for them to pay a fee for this facility and a typical sum is £15 - £20 but it could vary depending on your area. It may be that your cleaners will charge a fee to rearrange their cleaning rota. In order to clean a particular unit first, they are likely to now have to work a less efficient route around town. If you provide an M&G service, you will be asking your team member (or it might be you) to meet the guests at the property later than the scheduled time. It would therefore be appropriate to pay the M&G person extra to do this out of hours work, and the cost would need to be passed on to the guest. If neither of these are the case, it could be a good additional income stream for you.

Often when we inform the guest that there is going to be a fee for an early or late check in, or late checkout the guest cancels the request. In the event of a guest who hasn't paid for a late check in, if there is an M&G service, we would use our discretion on whether to charge a late check in fee depending on the circumstance. If the guest is late due to unforeseen circumstances, we are likely to waive the fee. If the guest is late and there is no way they could have made the check in on time due to the travel time they allowed and they opted out of paying a late check in fee when informed, we would charge the fee.

Same Day Bookings

Depending on your business model you may choose to allow same day bookings, which means you need to have your pre check in processes very slick. Up until what time at night can a potential guest book? If they book at 11.30pm are you going to be able to get your terms and conditions signed, and a copy of the guest ID sent through? If you do M&G will you be able to get someone to attend the property late at night? Some SA operators choose not to make their units available to be booked same day, which is done via the settings on your channel manager (see section on channel manager) or your OTA listing. The combination of same day bookings and one-night stays could be challenging for your cleaning team as a booking could come in late at night and the clean could be due the very next morning. Cleaners are such an important part of your business and plenty of notice of cleans will make running their business so much easier, which means if you have good cleaners, you are more likely to keep them!

#12. Business Structure

Every single person has a completely different tax status and therefore you should speak to a property accountant to establish how best to set up your SA business. It will be determined by your strategy for your SA business, but also by other income and businesses you already have. A common way to set up an SA business is to separate the operating entity from the owning entity/entities in order to maximise operational efficiency and tax benefits and to minimise business risk and limit personal liability.

Operating Company

There are a number of reasons to use a Limited Company (Ltd Co.), rather than operate in your own name. A Ltd Co. is an organisation you set up to run your business which is a completely separate entity to you (and any business partners). Everything from the company bank account to operational responsibility is separate from the interests of the company owners, i.e. the shareholders.

Contracts with landlords, letting agents, and suppliers such as cleaning and laundry companies etc. will usually be with the Ltd Co. In this instance, the operating company would not have any assets in it which means that if anyone were to slip up and injure themselves in the shower for instance, they would claim against your operating company's insurance and not go after assets as they are owned elsewhere. A Ltd Co. cannot protect an operator from criminal negligence, which is why it is so important to ensure that you and your properties are as safe and compliant as possible.

If you take a property from a letting agent on a rent to serviced accommodation (R2SA) basis, through a company let or a business lease to be used in your accommodation business, you will need to have a Ltd Co. to be able to do this.

Many Corporate Accommodation Agents will only use providers operating under a Ltd Co. structure, so to maximise your chance of getting reservations from them, you will need your own Ltd Co.

Operating through a Ltd Co. can provide a more professional image. You may find in addition to the agents mentioned already, you will get more direct bookings from companies based on a perception that service will be better and more reliable from a company than a Sole Trader.

Owning Entity

Not to be confused with the Operating Entity, there are different ways you could OWN property, as a Sole Trader (ST), in a Limited Liability Partnership (LLP) or in a Ltd Co. This may be property you already own, or property you subsequently buy.

Sole Trader

A Sole Trader operates under their own name, they need to complete a tax return and can be VAT registered, but unlike a Ltd Co., they are fully liable for any claims regarding money or accidents for example.

LLP

An LLP is a registered agreement between two or more individuals to take joint responsibility for the business including losses and expenditure and each partner pays tax on their own share of the profits. LLPs can also be made up of one person and a company, not just two or more individuals. An advantage with an LLP is that the partners are not personally liable for any debts the business can't pay.

Ltd Co.

A Ltd Co. can have certain tax advantages such as reducing personal tax, by shareholders receiving a small salary and the remainder of their income via dividends. There is a small amount of dividends that can be paid tax free. Shareholders are not personally liable for any losses made by the business. When people joint venture (JV) on a property project, often a Ltd Co. is used as a special purpose vehicle (SPV) for the purchase to ensure the project the JV partners are doing together is financially and legally separated from their other financial interests. A Ltd Co. provides each JV partner visibility and control on the day to day running of the company, where each partner's financial interests are properly recorded and accounted for using share holdings.

I would strongly advise taking the advice from an accountant or financial adviser who is experienced in SA, on what would be the most tax efficient way to buy property to use as SA. The main point to make here is that because SA is still relatively unknown, most accountants do not have the complete knowledge to give the right advice on how to buy property and the main reason is they do not fully understand the significance of SA Capital Allowances, and if they did they might give different advice. There are many aspects to consider when deciding which owning entity to choose, including tax planning, inheritance planning, funding and liability, but one aspect that must be a part of the decision making is how CAs can affect the amount of tax you pay.

Income from the first two entities (ST, LLP) will be taxed at your personal tax rate which will go up or down relative to your level of income including any salary you may have, or dividends paid from other companies etc. A Ltd Co. will pay Corporation Tax (CT) on profit which is calculated at the end of the financial year and paid the following year. Income from the Ltd Co. is taken as salary and dividends and you will pay tax on this money at your personal tax rate.

The owning entity also owns the CA, therefore, the amount of tax you are able to offset against a FHL capital allowance could be up to 45% if the property is owned personally or in an LLP, as opposed to the CT level which is 19% at the time of writing.

See 'Capital Allowances' section

#13. Professional Power Team

The following are key 'power team' members that you should have as part of your professional team of people to give you the right help and advice:

Capital Allowance Surveyor

As with all of your power team members one is not just as good as another. I once had a CA surveyor who said it was not worth submitting an SA claim for a particular property, whilst another returned a claim of £77,000, which represented a tax saving for me at the time of £33,800. Your accountant is not the right person to create your SA CA claim as he/she is not an expert in this field. You should consult with your CA surveyor in advance of being able to put in a CA claim because they will help you make decisions that will maximise your claim. In some scenarios the CA surveyor will need to create a claim to be accepted by all parties before exchange on a property otherwise a large percentage of the CA claim will be lost. By 'all parties' I mean the vendor selling the property and therefore their accountant and conveyancing solicitor, as well as your own accountant and conveyancing solicitor.

I do not want my power team members to be inundated with requests for free consultations and calls and so I give out their details to people who attend my training courses. Also, my power team changes from time to time, so I don't want to print the current contact information for that reason.

Commercial Energy Broker

SA property owners can pay commercial tariffs for their energy which is generally cheaper than domestic tariffs. There is VAT to be paid but even with VAT added it is often still cheaper to pay a commercial tariff. If your business becomes VAT registered and is on the standard rate scheme, you will be able to claim the VAT back on your energy costs. Switching to commercial energy is also a lot easier once you grow your business, because you will have one point of contact to deal with and not multiple energy suppliers who regularly send bills with no supply address listed as they are used to people only having one property and therefore only one bill.

Finance Broker

Your broker or brokers should be able to source SA specific borrowing across the whole spectrum of lenders. They will be critical when buying a property to use as SA and when replacing borrowing on existing BTLs or R2SA with a landlord.

Independent Ratings Surveyor

A rating surveyor is a very useful person to have on your side if you feel the Valuations Office Agency (VOA) is overcharging you for business rates. See also Business Rates v Council Tax section.

Property Accountant

It's imperative that you have an accountant with good SA knowledge because if not it could prove to be extremely expensive in terms of paying far too much tax. I am not suggesting any kind of tax evasion, it is simply about paying the appropriate amount of tax having set up your business correctly from the outset. There is no one size fits all scenario in terms of how you should set up and run your SA business for tax planning, because people with different individual financial circumstances are likely to get different advice from the same accountant.

SA Insurance Broker

Your broker needs to arrange the right cover for each SA property as well as cover for your operating company.

#14. Support Team

If you want to have a leveraged SA business, there are some people who are vital in your team. I will talk more about the main one here, your cleaning and housekeeping team which is without doubt the most important role in your entire SA business. Other roles that will be pivotal to you not creating another job for yourself are a virtual assistant (VA), personal assistant (PA), a meet and greet team (should you choose to go this route), at least one person to do reactive repairs (handyman) and some really reliable trades. If you scale you will also want to organise a bookkeeper unless you want to be bogged down in spreadsheets!

Cleaning and Housekeeping

It is crucial that you source cleaners who you are going to be able to work with for the months and years to come. Your initial meeting with your prospective cleaner is very important. You need to feel that you will be able to get along with him or her. You should trust your instincts on this because experience tells me that if you have your doubts about someone - you are right to have your doubts and you will probably regret it later on if you don't listen to your instincts.

The cleaning of your SAs is the biggest moving part in your business. As you grow your cleaners will need to grow with you. You therefore won't always be able to have the same cleaner every time and obviously some cleaners are going to be better than others. You will inevitably from time to time have the odd issue that needs to be resolved with your cleaners when the minimum standard of clean is not met. This might be down to the fact that the cleaning company are temporarily short staffed and had to rush that day to get all of their cleans done. It might be because they are training up a new cleaner who isn't yet up to standard when it comes to SA cleaning. Issues like this can be resolved and sometimes there can be some compromise between you and your cleaners to achieve it, but if your cleaners are not reasonable enough to understand when they need to raise their game then it's going to be a difficult relationship for a while until the inevitable happens and you have to source new cleaners. Bringing on new cleaners can be a disruptive transition because it takes a while for everything to run smoothly and so this should be avoided if at all possible, and this is why your initial instincts when you meet someone are so important.

To follow are some of the really important roles you need your housekeeping team to perform:

Check the Guest Key is Where it Should Be

If you are using physical keys, remember it is unlikely that you will be around when your guest departs and so you will probably tell the guests to put the keys in a specific place when they leave. This could be posting them through the letterbox of the property after locking the door or there might be a standalone letter box in a bank of boxes, which you often see in apartment blocks. Wherever it is that your guests are told to leave the keys, is vital that your cleaners confirm that they have been left there, and if they haven't, they must inform you ASAP so that you can contact the guest who has just left and if necessary arrange for a spare set of keys for your next guests.

If verifying the location of the keys is not done by your cleaners and the guest didn't put the keys where you asked them to, or left with them, then your next guests or the M&G team will not find the keys where they should be. In either case, missing keys will cause last minute hassle for you, your team and your guests.

Check the Heating

Many of our properties have heating controls that can be set remotely over WIFI and this is by far the best solution for controlling the central heating. If the heating is set from inside the property only, then this will need to be checked and put back to the regular settings by the cleaners. Often guests will put heating on constant and so this needs to be addressed. As with the other reasons listed here it is a good idea for your cleaners to clean as soon as possible on the day of check out to avoid unnecessary heating bills.

Bathroom Extractors Switched On

Firstly, it's very important to install extractor fans in bathrooms if your properties don't have them. Your cleaners should check that they are switched on as many guests choose to switch them off which will cause a build-up of condensation and mould. If the extractor is too noisy or operates for too long on a timer you should have this rectified because this will be why your guests are turning them off. One solution is to have extractors that operate when there is humidity in the air and not just because the light switch has been turned on. The other problem with light switch operated extractor fans is that in the summer months guests may not switch the lights on.

Damaged/Missing/Broken

Although it is rare, any damage needs to be flagged up to you immediately. This is so that you can raise it with your guest and if necessary, arrange how they would like to pay for the damage, i.e. should you take it out of the deposit, charge their card or would they like to pay by bank transfer. A significant delay in contacting the guest is going to create a scenario whereby the guest is more likely to challenge if it was indeed their party who caused the damage. This is one of the reasons that you always want your cleans to take place the same day as a check out and as soon as possible after a check out. The cleaner should have the ability to take a photo (usually on their smartphone) of the damage and send it to you. There are many cost-effective ways of sending photos but things inevitably change over time, so for that reason I won't recommend these options but as with anything you can *google* it, and as I am writing this I am wondering how long '*Google* it' will be a thing!

I will cover WIFI later, but if your cleaner pairs with your WIFI they will be able to send you photos for free over the WIFI. I will also cover reviews later but it's worth mentioning here that falling out with a guest over some minor damage is not worth getting a bad review over because bad reviews will cost you money in the long run. You have to consider the fact that the 'lead guest' who made the initial booking is going to be the person you call, and that person might genuinely not know that someone else in the party caused some damage. You should be as tactful and polite as possible when you call and always give them the benefit of the doubt unless it would be impossible for them not to know.

If something is damaged, you need to decide on what to do and this decision usually revolves around when your next guest is due to arrive. If it can be fixed in time so be it, but if not and the damage will have a significant impact on your next guest, like a broken bed, you will need to take some action to get on top of the situation. In an ideal world you will have one or two options (the greater the number the better) of handymen to call and hopefully one of them will be able to come and fix the problem. If not and you have more than one SA, you could move the guests there. A nice way of phrasing the change of location it is to offer a complimentary upgrade. If you are not able to offer an alternative yourself then you can always contact the other SA operators locally and see if any of them can accommodate the booking and you simply transfer the money to them and if necessary, pay the difference. Hopefully there won't be too much of a difference bearing in mind that the other operator would not need to pay a commission on the booking to an OTA and therefore should be able to offer an equivalent discount. They might even be able to do it cheaper bearing in mind that they probably thought that they were not going to get a booking at all as they were clearly not already booked and so some money in the bank is better than no money in the bank!

Inventory

You also need to know if minor things are missing like cutlery, plates, cups, and glasses etc, because over time these get broken or simply go missing and you don't want to find out by reading a negative review that there was only one fork for a family of four. It's good to have spare stock of these types of item so that it can be easily sorted out. We buy things in bulk not only to get a cost saving but also so that we can replace things with like for like items.

TV Remote

It's important to check that your TV remote is present and the batteries work. Another key thing to check is that the TV menus are set to English as some guests will change the TV settings to their own language, and so you should show your cleaners how to change it back to English. We first did this using '*google* translate' once we had confirmed the nationality of the previous guest. It's easier to write out some instructions for your cleaner whilst the settings are displayed in English. These instructions can be left in the 'guest manual' that I will cover later with other user guides and instructions for your guests and cleaners to refer to. If the TV remote is missing whether lost down the side of the sofa, accidentally thrown out with the rubbish or taken by your guests, I recommend having a spare 'all in one' remote that you keep in the property but not accessible to your guests unless required.

Minor Faults/Repairs

Your cleaners are the most likely people on your team to spot that things need to be fixed. This could be something like a window that doesn't close properly because it's dropped a little or the toilet cistern doesn't fill very quickly. If things like this aren't flagged up to you and fixed the first time you will know about it is from a bad review. It's important to check that light bulbs are working, and I advise that you have plenty of spares at the property so that your cleaner can change the blown ones for you.

Replenish Your Welcome Pack

Most SAs provide tea/coffee, milk, sugar in the kitchen and some soap/shower gel/shampoo in the bathrooms/toilets in a welcome pack for each guest, similar to what you might expect to find in a hotel. You can keep the spare stock in your lockable cupboard or box. In some properties where we don't have a cupboard, we use a plastic box that can be opened using a combination (not given to the guests). The best people to restock your welcome pack for your next guests are your cleaners.

Clean/Dirty Linen

You need to arrange/coordinate with your cleaner on how and where to drop off your used linen (towels, sheets etc.) and where to collect the clean. The cleaning company might have a base or office where the laundry company can drop off the clean and collect the dirty, or if not, you will need to establish where and how this is going to happen. An outside store or shed could work but please ensure that it is a clean and dry place and that it doesn't have any little furry four legged creatures also frequenting the establishment or indeed living there on a permanent basis! Some cleaners also offer to launder and press your linen for you and if this is the case then storing the linen is going to be their concern. It is worth bearing in mind that this arrangement might work for a while, but as you scale up your cleaner is unlikely to be able to cope with the volume and so it might be worthwhile switching to a commercial laundry company sooner rather than later.

So these are the main things that you should ask your cleaner to do for you, and this should be made clear when they are quoting for your business, because if you ask them to do this retrospectively, they may understandably raise their prices or simply say no. There will undoubtedly be some initial teething problems that you need to work through with your cleaners, but if you have entered into a business relationship with good people from the outset, this should not require too much effort.

Alan Bond –
MiPAD Bath

66 When we first saw the Midford Mill, I didn't like it; grade II listed, had flooded 3 times in the last 10 years, was run-down and neglected, and the best part of a million pounds asking price! But the other partners loved it. It took me 3 visits to finally see that it could work. It could sleep 10-12 at a time, and a quick search of the local Bath area told me there was little competition in properties of this size, especially one set in such beautiful countryside on the southern edge of one of the UK's most iconic and visited cities. With over 1 million overnight stays per year Bath is a great place to do Serviced Accommodation.

Being engineers we looked at the problems. It didn't take us long to work out why the building was flooding so regularly. It wasn't down to location or design, the building had been there since the 1600s. It was pure mismanagement from an owner that simply did not understand how to look after such a property. With this insight we looked at ways to make it work for us.

From my training and mentorship with Kevin, I understood the reliefs and legal ways of reducing the overheads associated with buying and financing such a venture, including £200k of Capital Allowances! We also knew from a study of the market that we could easily get £1500 for a weekend.

We secured the property for £840k, some £110k below current asking price, and £260k below the purchase price 7 years earlier. The flooding issue had put everyone off and we were the only bidders 'foolish' enough to make an offer. By November the property was ours and we set about overhauling it. In truth most of the work was cosmetic but there were ceilings falling down, damp and rotten timbers to sort, again all from mismanagement rather than structural issues.

We were unable to find any local builders we could trust and ended up doing most of the work ourselves (a bad example of leverage!). Once the property was ready to go live as a single SA dwelling, we welcomed our first guests as we were driving to France to go skiing! We were therefore not around so had to rely on the systems we had put in place. It took us 3 sets of cleaners before we found our rhythm (we are now on our fourth set). It became clear very early on that your cleaners are the most important part of any SA system. They are your eyes and ears, if you want a hands-off business, and need careful selection.

We sorted the flooding issues and put a flood management plan in place. We then got this assessed by a specialist company. Their letter sanctioning our actions allowed us to reduce our insurance premium from £5000 pa (with a £50k excess!) to normal terms, which more importantly, gave us access to all lenders as opposed to just a choice of two. We could now re-finance and extract our money. The property was subsequently valued at £1.25M. Re-financing allowed us to find and finance the follow-on property which went live in Sep this year.

Two years on and the mill is proving as popular as ever. We forecast a turnover of £50k in year one. We actually turned over £86k. This year that will be even higher. We are running at about 55% profit on turnover. We still have to work hard to fill mid-week and are now focused on improving our 62% occupancy rate.

In short, we love The Mill and we love Serviced Accommodation. We are now sourcing property number 5.

Before   *After*

#15. Compliance

Insurance

The short-term rental market is a completely different insurance risk to BTL, so you need to ensure you have a suitable building and contents insurance policy. Your policy will need to include Public Liability to cover you against accidents or injury to your guests, Loss of Rent (SA income), Employers Liability to cover people employed at your property, Accidental Damage and Theft Cover. You are likely to also need Professional Indemnity (PI) insurance to cover you against allegations of misrepresentation in your marketing. PI can also protect you against a claim from another company claiming a loss of income due to the business relationship or contract with your company.

For the same reason as with my accountant, I give the details of my broker to the people who attend my training courses, but if you were sourcing your own broker, you should ensure that they have clients who also have an SA business and don't just take their word for it. Client confidentiality rules apply here but ask the broker if their current SA clients would be happy for you to contact them for a chat. If the broker is forthcoming it should give you the confidence to proceed with them.

Housing & Health & Safety Rating System (HHSRS)

For England and Wales, if you enter HHSRS into your browser it will give you the current guidance for people providing accommodation. For Scotland enter Housing Act 2006 Scotland. For Northern Ireland enter health and safety rented accommodation Northern Ireland.

Data Protection and Payment Card Industry (PCI) Compliance

As per the General Data Protection Regulation (GDPR) if you are holding or capturing any customer information like name, address, contact details etc. then you will need to be registered with the Information Commissioner's Office (ICO). The ICO will provide you with the guidelines to follow in order to be compliant and at the time of writing, it is £40 per year to register and they provide lots of helpful information. If you intend to market to your guests you must ensure you have a legal right to do so, the most common reason being you have the customer's consent. The rules around this got tighter with the introduction of GDPR so you will need to read up on this in order to make sure you remain compliant.

Payment Card Industry (PCI) compliance is also important for businesses taking card payments from consumers. If you are using a channel manager and/or a card channel manager (see relevant section) those organisations will be handling the customers' card data on your behalf, so you should ensure that they are PCI Compliant.

You should never store customer data and card details on paper or anywhere that could be accessed by a third party.

Lease Restrictions

For leasehold properties it is important to check that the lease allows short lets to take place in the property. Every lease is different and there is not much case law around this at the time of writing. The cases that have been brought to the courts have not been black and white in their ruling. Some leases will be drawn up to allow owner occupiers only which even prohibits letting to a tenant on an AST. Others will allow subletting but only for six month ASTs or longer. In these cases, short term lettings are not allowed and operating as such would be a breach of the lease conditions. An AST is not the correct contract to use for an SA guest because it should not be their principal private residence and an AST is designed for tenants not guests.

If a leaseholder is breaching the terms and conditions of a lease, the freeholder can revoke the lease and effectively repossess the property. This is only likely to happen if the lease does in fact prohibit short lets, the SA operator refuses to cease the SA activity when told to by the management company on behalf of the freeholder, and where the freeholder is willing to take legal action. My advice is to check if it is allowed in the first place and ask a property solicitor if you are unsure of the terminology, but if you are already doing SA in your leasehold property, which after checking you discover SA is not permitted, and the freeholder or management company tell you to stop short letting, then simply stop. Many blocks of flats have a lease that doesn't actually allow SA, but SA has been taking place for years there without issue and there are several in operation. It boils down to the fact that some freeholders and block management companies are strict on this and some are not, but in my opinion it's always best to be on the safe side.

Mortgages/Loans

If you decide to begin doing SA on a property and it has an existing mortgage or loan, it is important to check whether SA is allowed within the mortgage or loan terms and conditions (more likely with a commercial loan). If it currently is not you should get permission from the lender before commencing SA activity.

If you cannot get permission, you could replace the existing mortgage/loan with an SA specific product. If that is not possible, at the time of writing one of my mortgage brokers is able to arrange a 'Bridge to Let' loan which is less than 7% interest per annum in total. This product is designed for 'newbie' operators who after one or two years of operation in SA, have shown that they are running their SA business well and the same lender will replace the bridging with an SA specific mortgage which is currently at a slightly higher interest rate than a BTL mortgage would be.

See R2SA for more info/advice

#16. Tax

I do not intend to go into too much detail in this section because tax is forever changing and there is never a definitive course of action to take because individual circumstances only need to differ slightly for there to be a different tax strategy. My advice is to seek guidance from an experienced SA accountant, as well as refer to HMRC for more information.

Serviced Accommodation (SA) V Furnished Holiday Let (FHL)

As far as HMRC and the planning department are concerned SA is more like a hotel, guest house or B&B where there are certain services available to guests such as 24 hr concierge, on site bar/restaurant, room service and laundry service and most accommodation like this is C1 use class. FHL is similar in that it provides furnished short stay accommodation, with all of the utilities provided in the cost of the booking. Services are provided such as pre and post stay clean and fresh bedding and towels, but FHL would usually be fully self-catering and there would be no 'on site' staff. Most properties operated as FHL are C3 (residential) use class. An often-raised question that I would like to clear up here is that a FHL does not have to be situated in a 'recognised holiday location', it just has to meet certain qualifying criteria as dictated by HMRC and central/local government.

As I said at the beginning of this book, some confusion arises because many people use the term Serviced Accommodation when referring to both FHL and SA. When people look for books, podcasts and training courses to learn how to invest in FHL and SA they will predominantly use the term Serviced Accommodation as their search words. For that reason, I have called this book Serviced Accommodation Success, my Podcast is called the Serviced Accommodation Property Podcast and my training courses are also referred to as Serviced Accommodation training.

Furnished Holiday Let (FHL) Qualifying Criteria.

Many people in the UK doing what is known colloquially as 'Serviced Accommodation' are actually doing FHL as far as HMRC is concerned. To qualify as FHL a property should be available commercially for short term lettings for 210 days in a year and let for a minimum of 105 but stays of longer than 31 days cannot form part of the 105. The 105 days of short lets must consist of bookings of 31 days or less, and stays of 31 or more days must not exceed 155 days in a year.

If you have more than one SA and one of them falls short of the 105 days of bookings in the year, you can opt for an 'averaging election' in order to get all the SAs to qualify. The way this works is if you add up the total number of days booked across all SAs in that business, then divide the total bookings by the number of SAs in the business. If the result is 105 days or more, then the property that fell below the threshold will now also qualify.

For example:

The SA operator lets four SAs for the following number of days in a year:

SA1	120 days
SA2	125 days
SA3	112 days
SA4	64 days
Total	**421 days**

Using averaging election, all four SAs will meet the letting condition (421 days divided by 4 SAs = 105 days per property). Without averaging election, SA4 would not have qualified, but do remember, you can only average across properties in a single SA business.

The qualification year for a new SA starts from when it becomes operational and for a continuing unit, it will default to the tax year - that is from 6 April one year to 5 April in the next. When FHL activity stops, apply the tests to the 12 months up to when the bookings finish.

Value Added Tax (VAT)

Income from SA is subject to VAT, whereas income from BTL and HMO is not. When the owning entity reaches the current VAT threshold then VAT is chargeable to customers and therefore payable to HMRC on the total turnover received. A standard VAT bill is calculated as VAT charged minus VAT paid on bills to run the business known as input VAT. Please refer to the HMRC website for the current VAT thresholds and charges.

This is particularly important for SA operators as the market dictates the maximum night rate they can charge, so when they need to charge VAT to a customer, they can't simply add VAT to the price, otherwise the customer will book elsewhere. A proportion of the income becomes payable to HMRC, reducing the overall profit.

As previously stated for asset protection reasons, most people operate using a Ltd Co. which owns no assets, and this company will have its own VAT threshold. If this company charges Management fees to you or your clients, it will have to start charging VAT when its revenue reaches the threshold.

In addition, each different owning entity legitimately has its own VAT threshold subject to the criteria mentioned below in the Artificial Separation section. If you buy or own property in your own name and use it as SA, then you personally have your own VAT threshold. If you buy or own property in an LLP or Ltd Co. and use it as SA, then that entity has its own VAT threshold.

Artificial Separation

In terms of tax planning it is essential that you understand what constitutes a legitimate separation of VAT eligible entities. Sometimes the people I train ask if they can simply split their business into smaller chunks, i.e. have a separate entity for each property. This is not advisable, as business owners who separate their business into separate parts in order to stay under the VAT threshold and avoid VAT registration, can be subject to HMRC fines or prosecution, as this is seen as a form of tax evasion. There are specific rules set out by HMRC which means you must prove there is no financial, economic or organisational link between your businesses, to avoid what is known as artificial separation. HMRC are very strict on artificial separation and you should seek advice from your accountant to ensure you don't fall foul of this. There is a lot of guidance around this on the Government website at the time of writing, search "VAT Single Entity and Disaggregation" for the latest information and checklists.

VAT Schemes

There are different VAT schemes applicable to different business models and your accountant will need to advise you on which one is right for you and your business.

Tour Operators Margin Scheme (TOMS)

This system is designed for businesses where services are put together as a package for customers and under certain circumstances this applies to R2SA. The operator must lease the accommodation and they must contract directly with the guest, i.e. not as a managing agent. The TOMS scheme allows the operator to only pay VAT on the margin between their revenue and the costs of running the business, including the lease costs for the property. The TOMS scheme therefore allows the rent being paid to the owner to be deducted as an allowable cost. This will significantly reduce the VAT payable.

Flat Rate Scheme

Before hitting the VAT threshold, if your SA business qualifies (get advice from your accountant), you can opt to go on to the flat rate scheme. You can do this via the HMRC website, or your accountant will do it for you. At the time of writing the flat rate scheme for SA is 9.5% for the first year of operation and 10.5% thereafter. You will then be paying 9.5/10.5% VAT on your turnover and you will not be able to claim back any input VAT tax, which is the VAT you have paid out to run your business such as your cleaning and laundry invoices. The main benefit of being on the scheme is there will be less administration and accounting required because there will be no need to calculate the difference between VAT charged to customers and VAT paid to suppliers.

The one proviso here is that your business could be classed as a 'Limited Cost business' if your relevant costs are too low compared to your turnover (less than 2% or £1000). You will then need to pay a higher rate of VAT, i.e. 15.5% for the first year followed by 16.5%.

Once registered you can reclaim VAT on 'goods' up to three years prior to registration and 'services' up to six months.

Standard Rate

Once your projected turnover reaches the upper limit of the Flat Rate Scheme (£230,000 Inc. VAT in 2019) you will need to move to the Standard Rate. On this scheme you calculate the VAT payable to the HMRC as the difference between VAT charged and VAT paid.

As with the Flat Rate, once registered you can reclaim VAT on 'goods' up to three years prior to registration and 'services' up to six months.

The Reduced Value Rule

The full amount of VAT only needs to be paid on the first 28 days of a booking, and from day 29 onwards you do not have to pay VAT on the accommodation portion of the booking, only the services part. Unfortunately, the reduced value rule is not allowed if you have a corporate client making a block booking, i.e. over 29 days, even though each person they send to you stays for less than 29 days.

Section 24

The Section 24 tax legislation that was introduced in the UK 2015 budget dictated that BTL and HMO landlords would no longer be able to offset their mortgage interest against rental income and tax relief would be limited to 20% where previously there was no cap. The net result of this is to make it appear that a landlord is generating more income from the property (the amount of the mortgage interest) and their tax will be calculated based on that artificially inflated income. As a result of this inflated income, it is predicted that hundreds of thousands of UK landlords will become higher rate taxpayers because of Section 24, and many of them will actually start making a loss from their investment properties where previously they were making a profit. As a result, many property investors now choose to buy property in a Ltd Co. because as such, mortgage/loan interest can still be offset against income before tax is calculated.

The main drawback of a Ltd Co. setup is extra admin and accountancy costs and in order to take the money out of the Ltd Co. bank account, dividend tax has to be paid, which at the time of writing can be as high as 38.1%, having already paid corporation tax, currently 19%, on the profits. One of the main reasons that SA is such a great strategy right now is that mortgage interest can still be offset against SA income subject to meeting the FHL or SA criteria. Therefore, there is no need to buy SA property, or property destined for SA use, via a Ltd Co. in order to avoid Section 24 tax.

Capital Allowances (CAs)

CAs are an amount of money HMRC allows you to earn without paying tax providing that the CAs haven't been claimed by the previous owner. They are reliefs that can be set against taxable profits reducing the amount of tax you pay. If a property has never been used as SA before i.e. it has always been a residential property, then a claim could not have been made as the property would not have been eligible to claim CAs.

CAs are not available on property when used as BTL or HMO or a private residence i.e. your home where there is no SA activity. Most people, and their accountants, do not know much about claiming CAs on SA, which is why most eligible SA property have not had a claim because it is underestimated how much a potential CA claim can be.

In terms of a definitive description of CAs, the obvious place is the legislation, Capital Allowances Act 2001, which can be viewed on the government's website, but It's a bit heavy going. You should be aware that CAs cover a number of different tax reliefs, the most common one is Plant & Machinery Allowances. Plant & Machinery covers such things in an SA as lighting, heating, power supplies, sanitary ware, kitchen installations, swimming pools and air-conditioning units.

There is some extra compliance work for the CA surveyor to do but the basic process is:

- Identify if any of the prior owners have claimed any CAs

- Check the tax history of the property

- Review sale/purchase contracts

- Undertake a site survey to identify the value of plant and machinery

Commercial property and SA can claim significant CAs. If a developer does a commercial conversion, such as turning offices into flats, or new build into houses or apartments and sells the units on, CAs cannot be claimed because they have 'disposed' of the asset. Similarly, if they hold the property and use it for BTL use, they will not be able to claim CAs, apart from a relatively small claim in the communal areas of an apartment block. If, however, the developer builds or converts into residential property and it is subsequently used as SA, they will be able to submit a substantial CA claim on the whole development.

The claim is based loosely on a percentage of the purchase price of a property, and a percentage of the cost of the refurbishment work that has taken place on the property, which will form the total expenditure. Claims will clearly vary property to property, but good CA surveyors tell me that they are typically able to create a claim which represents 30-35% of total expenditure. So, with a house being used as SA with a total expenditure of £200,000, let's say the claim is £65,000. This means that the SA operator would be able to earn 65K from their SA business tax free. Any CA that has not been claimed will roll over into the next tax year until used up. Once the CA is used there is no claw back from HMRC if SA activity stops or the property is sold. Once the CAs are used up, tax is paid on profit at the appropriate rate of the individual or company.

A point to note is that it is the 'owning entity' of a property that owns the CA. This means that if the property is owned by a Ltd Co. it would be that owning entity that qualifies for the CA and Ltd Co. will save corporation tax. If a person owns a property in their own name or with other people in an LLP, that person or those partners will qualify for the CA and will therefore save income tax. Once a property has been available as FHL for at least 210 days and has had 105 days worth of bookings, it is possible to submit a CA claim. SA and hotel/guest house type property can claim on day one of SA activity.

You should be aware that any CAs identified for a FHL can only be used against your FHL business. If you own commercial properties such as a hotel (or a hotel whose rooms are offered as studio flats), HMRC deem this to be SA and those CAs can be used against ANY other taxable income under the sideways loss relief rules (check your eligibility with a knowledgeable accountant), but FHL allowances are ring fenced (since 2012) to the FHL business. Either scenario will significantly reduce the amount of tax you pay!

Business Rates v Council Tax

Different Councils seem to apply different rules on this issue but overall, FHL and SA should be on Business Rates. Many local councils however do not actually want FHL (whole house or apartment SA) going over to Business Rates because they will lose the Council Tax revenue. Small Business Rates Relief (SBRR), which at the time of writing gives full relief up to £12,000 PA on business rates, means that most FHL operators would not need to pay council tax or business rates on at least one property within the SA business!

The person in your local council who actually works for HMRC as part of the Valuations Office Agency (VOA) is the person who will assess the tax for your business. Business rates are calculated on the Rateable Value Per Unit (RVU) x Single Bed Spaces (SBS) x Multiplier or Uniform Business Rate (UBR) which differs per area. A double bed would count as 2 x SBS. The business rates qualifying criteria states that the property should be available as FHL for 140 days. In Wales the property should be available for 140 days and actually occupied by guests for 70 days.

I do sometimes hear that a VOA officer has overestimated the business rates payable on a FHL. You can challenge this via the HMRC website although it would be worth consulting with your VOA first to try to resolve it. If you still don't get this resolved, you can appoint an independent ratings surveyor who will use his or her expert knowledge to work on your behalf in order to lower your business rates to the correct level. A ratings surveyor I spoke to recently told me that in his opinion currently 80% of FHLs would pay either the same or less than council tax if they had the correct business rates valuation.

You will be able to claim SBRR on at least one FHL but If you have more than one FHL, it would be wise to claim it on the FHL with the most bed spaces because that will generate the biggest tax saving. Therefore, you could end up paying no Council Tax or business rates on your most expensive property. If you are in the 20% where you are paying more in business rates than Council Tax, the SBRR saving will either cover the extra expenditure or significantly offset it depending on the size of your FHL portfolio and where it is. In any case the extra income generated from a well-run FHL portfolio should make it worthwhile.

The following excerpt is provided by a Ratings Surveyor:

"Quite simply - Serviced Accommodation (SA) is a commercial operation, and as a result a property operated as SA should be entered into the non-domestic rating list (business rates).

Non-domestic rating (business rates) is valued as rebus sic stantibus – which means that the Valuation Office Agency (VOA) will value it as it stands, i.e. the property will be valued for the use in which it is being operated, which may not be the same use as the planning consent. Rating and planning do not necessarily have a relationship.

This is not to say that, as an SA operator, you necessarily want your property to fall under business rating, as there are situations where if an existing residential property is to be operated as SA and already has a Council Tax assessment, it may be beneficial to leave it on Council Tax. This depends on several factors which I will discuss below.

When it comes to the business rates or Council Tax dilemma, it needs to be understood that if you decide to leave a property under Council Tax, and the VOA discover it is being used as SA, they have a statutory duty to investigate and to take the correct action, which can include back dating.

How likely is it that the VOA will find out? Well, how long is a piece of string? In most cases the chances of the VOA discovering residential property being operated as SA are quite low. That said some local authorities have inspectors and researchers who might pick up on it by trawling through the likes of Booking.com and Airbnb, and if they do, they are duty bound to report it to the VOA for them to look at. In addition, if the VOA are notified by an operator who operates an apartment as SA in a block of say 200 apartments, they may take it upon themselves to look to see if any other apartments in the same development are operated as SA.

It is key to understand that there is not a "one size fits all" approach as to which route should be taken. Every situation needs looking at individually as to the likely Rateable Value under business rating, what the payable rates would be and the situation with any reliefs, such as small business rate relief. Strategy is very important when it comes to rating, be it domestic or non-domestic.

How does the VOA value SA? Left to their own devices, most offices of the VOA will place a value per single bed space, so a double is two single bed spaces, a two double bedroom property four single bed spaces etc., which is the same method of valuation as self-contained holiday accommodation (FHL).

It is important to point out at this point, that the Rateable Value of a property is not what you will pay. You will pay a percentage of the Rateable Value, depending on the Uniform Business Rate (UBR) for the financial year. The UBR for 2018/19 was £0.48 for smaller rating assessments (up to £20,000 outside London), and £0.493 for larger rating assessments. The UBR changes every financial year and is linked to inflation.

Many operators can take advantage of the benefits of small business rate relief. At the time of writing, If an operator only has liability for one property, and the Rateable Value is less than £12,000, then the operator will qualify for 100% small business rate relief and will not pay anything. The scheme also tapers so that there is partial relief for Rateable Values between £12,000-£15,000. There is further potential for additional properties to benefit from the relief as any additional properties with a Rateable Value of £2,899 or less, up to a maximum total of £20,000 (£25,000 in London) will also qualify.

Strategy is all important when it comes to small business rate relief. Every legal entity qualifies for relief. So, for example a Ltd Co. is a legal entity, as is a Sole Trader, as is a Partnership, an LLP etc. So, it is possible to set your operation up to make the most of small business rate relief, such as operating more than one Ltd Co., or operating some property in a Ltd Co., some as a Sole Trader, some in a Partnership etc (author insert – please take an accountants advice to ensure you are not creating artificial separation scenario for tax).

I will take this opportunity to reiterate that it is vitally important when thinking about business rates to be as sure as you can be about the likely Rateable Value of a property. Let's take London - a two double-bedroomed apartment may be valued by the VOA at say £2,000 per single bed space, so a Rateable Value of £8,000. The UBR for 2018/19 was £0.48 for small

Rateable Values so the payable rates would be £3,840 per annum. The Council Tax charge for the same property may be less than half that amount. Of course, if the property was your only SA unit within the legal entity it would qualify for small business rate relief and business rates would work very well. It is important to note here that I have seen values of up to £6,000 per single bed space in upmarket areas of Central London so caution needs to be exercised.

Another example - say you operate five one-bedroom apartments in a large development on the outskirts of Leeds. Each apartment totals two single bed spaces which are likely to be valued at circa £750 each. A Rateable Value of £1,500 per apartment. The first apartment would qualify for full small business rate relief and as the other four apartments have Rateable Values of less than £2,899 and the total of all five assessments would be £7,500 (less than £20,000 total), the additional apartments would also qualify for full relief and no rates would be payable, whereas Council Tax on the 5 apartments would have likely cost £6,000 per annum.

A third and final example, a large pub conversion in a low value area of the North West of England converted into 21 rooms, all double bedrooms and en-suite. The total cost of Council Tax had the VOA gone down that route, which they could have done without being "steered" would have been circa £24,000 per annum. Under Business Rates at £900 per single bed space, a Rateable Value of £37,800. The UBR for larger assessments such as this for 2018/19 is £0.493, so the rating liability for 2018/19 would be £18,635.4 – which would you rather pay?"

You get the picture from the information and examples above, that business rating is a complex area, and caution needs to be exercised, but with the right approach, strategy and research it can be advantageous, depending on the specific circumstances. There has been a lot in the press recently about business rates reform and potential replacement taxes. The fact is that the treasury receives £26BN per annum from business rates and as a tax it isn't going to disappear any time soon.

The person responsible for paying the business rates is the person who should apply for it along with the SBRR. So in a R2SA situation, the SA operator applies for and pays the business rates, whereas in a management situation, the owner applies for and pays the business rates.

Andrew and Clare Ferguson –
Penstar Locations Holiday Rental
and Serviced Accommodation

" Our property strategy to buy distressed properties, refurb, refinance and then rent, creating a solid income was working well, but the whole effort meant we would not achieve the financial freedom we were aiming for anytime soon. That's when Clare said she had seen this guy Kevin Poneskis speak and a property seminar and suggested I go on one of his Serviced Accommodation courses. Within 12 weeks I had attended the Discovery Day, the Serviced Accommodation Intensive two day course and the Mastermind and we'd launched our first Rent to SA.

We decided that our next refurb project would be launched as an SA unit and when tenants moved out of one of the two rentals we have outside of the Limited Company we jumped at the chance to beat Section 24 and once again claim mortgage costs as business costs. Along with a long standing holiday let we have in Cape Town, we launched an interesting little mix of properties in our SA portfolio.

Being a good soldier, I always followed instructions from Kevin, although I normally grumbled a bit about costs and made some sceptical noises, but these were all good, particularly when we came to the bigger items like Capital Allowances and Small Business Rates Exemption.

Kevin was very insistent that we would find Capital Allowances beneficial, so OK I said I would have a go (grumbling about cost and chances of success). we contacted one of Kevin's go to CA surveyors and provided various pieces of information, and to my surprise we were able to secure an allowance of circa £30k. That's an awful lot of tax free revenue on just one small unit, not surprisingly I am now looking at CAs for the second property (we looked at the Cape Town property but apparently CA is restricted to the EU).

Then there is the Small Business Rates Exemption, I love this one! So Kevin says 'stop dawdling Ferguson and pull your finger out', and off I went. By luck the 3 UK properties were all held in different legal entities which meant we could request that each one was converted from Council Tax to Business Rates and then made exempt on the basis of being a small single unit business, this one blew me away, saving circa £4.5K per annum straight to the bottom line profit in perpetuity.

There have been many little 'tricks of the trade' and nuances that Kevin has shared with me but these two in particular have been quite extraordinary. 🢱🢱

Rent a Room Allowance

At the time of writing the current allowance is £7,500. This allowance allows you to use part of your own home as SA and means that you can earn whatever the allowance is per annum tax free. Please remember that you can only claim this on your own home and not a 'stand-alone SA'. However, you are not allowed to offset expenditure which means that if you spend say £1,000 on a bed and some furniture and a TV for your 'SA room' in your house, you wouldn't be able to claim the cost of that back as well as having the tax free allowance.

This allowance is great because you can get your bookings, communicate with guests and receive payment using all of your existing systems, and many SA operators start their SA business by renting a room out in their own home first. It's also worth pointing out that many people can create a private annex in their home with its own entrance that provides security and privacy for the owner and guests alike and this allowance can still be claimed.

SECTION 4: ACQUISITION

The reason I have written 'acquisition' and not 'buy' is that there are more ways to acquire SA property other than simply to buy it. I will cover the main ones in this section.

#17. Rent to Serviced Accommodation (R2SA) Via a Landlord

Existing landlords are a good place to start when it comes to building your SA business. A major revelation is you don't have to own property yourself to earn significant money out of SA! You can simply rent it from someone else using an appropriate agreement (please seek legal advice) and use it as SA. If a landlord has a mortgage on the property, then they should get permission from the lender for it to be used as SA (Short Term Lettings). In my experience the lender is more likely to say yes if the term "Furnished Holiday Let" is used as opposed to "Serviced Accommodation," because more often than not the employee taking your call will not know what SA is. If a landlord is experiencing tenant voids and struggling to pay the mortgage, the lender is more likely to agree to the property being used as FHL. Sometimes this permission will be granted temporarily, but with no actual fixed date given for FHL activity to stop.

If the landlord doesn't ask the lender and the lender subsequently becomes aware that the property is being used as SA and the mortgage product does not allow it, I am aware of cases where the lender has told the owner to stop or increased the interest rate payable. If a lender is not willing to allow it, they will give a notice to stop, and If you do stop there is no further action. I am informed by people in the mortgage industry that the lender will only go down the route of calling in the loan if the owner refuses to stop. I would prefer for people not to take any chances on this and so my advice is that if a property has a mortgage on it, the lender should be consulted, and permission granted in advance.

I unequivocally advise that you never buy a property with a BTL or a residential (owner occupier) mortgage and immediately start using it as SA. Even if your initial intention was not to do SA with the house, it is likely to be deemed as mortgage fraud and you could not only have the loan called in and potentially lose the house, but you could also be 'black listed' by the Council of Mortgage Lenders and never be able to get another mortgage again.

So, if you are doing R2SA you should ask if there is a mortgage on the property, and if there is, you should inform the owner that they should seek permission from the mortgage lender. It's going to be very difficult for you to 'supervise' the owner to ensure that they have spoken to their lender so my advice is that you put it in writing that you have advised the landlord to inform and get permission from the lender and get them to sign that they have received this advice and permission has been granted. The gold-plated solution is that the owner gets it in writing from their lender that permission is granted, and you are given a copy.

I am happy to report that my mortgage broker informs me there are more and more SA products becoming available, so if permission isn't granted for SA, one option is to replace the existing mortgage with a tailor made one. At the time of writing the interest rate is slightly higher than most BTL mortgage rates, but if that's what it takes to get the deal done then so be it. You could also offer the owner a higher rent on the property to compensate for the higher mortgage cost. I have between 65% and 75% loan to value interest only SA mortgages as well as commercial repayment SA loans. My broker is also able to get loans/mortgages for 'newbie' SA investors, so the situation is definitely getting better as the demand for SA grows the lenders are stepping up to meet the demand. It's worth mentioning that 40% of property in the UK has no mortgage at all, so another simpler scenario would be that you do R2SA on mortgage free property!

There are three different strategies to deploy when deciding what rent level to pay. You can simply rent it from the owner at the normal BTL rate. You could even pay more than normal BTL rent if that's what it takes to get a really good SA property. By the same token, you can negotiate a discount because there are some significant advantages to the owner if the property is used as SA.

BENEFITS TO THE LANDLORD

Long Term Income with No Voids

As an experienced BTL landlord myself I know that voids can totally wipe out BTL profit. When a landlord is between tenants, they have to pay the mortgage and all the bills while getting no rent. They will more often than not have to pay a lot more than the tenant deposit amount to put the property back to immaculate condition. You can guarantee to pay the rent on time each month and keep the property in show home condition throughout. BTL landlords will not be used to that so you could be their ideal tenant!

Weekly Inspections

We recommend that even if you have a long-term guest that you do at least a weekly clean (and linen change) and as a result you will be able to promise weekly inspections of the property. Any maintenance issues will be flagged immediately which will eliminate the damage that can occur when tenants don't report an issue and small maintenance job turns into a major incident.

Maintenance

When it comes to maintenance and repairs, it is in your best interest as an SA operator to have the work done by your trusted tradespeople. A BTL landlord will have previously had to take calls from tenants then chase trades to go to the property to do the repairs. An objective financial incentive that you may or may not offer, is to take financial care of any minor maintenance, say any bill of under £50, but anything higher you will pass the cost to the landlord. You can negotiate a good rate for repeat work from your trades, which when you pass on applicable costs to the landlord, they are likely to be cheaper than they are used to and will therefore be value for money for them.

Low Risk

As you the operator are paying a fixed amount of rent and covering all the utility bills and running costs, there is no risk to the owner around seasonal income fluctuations and potential lack of demand. All of the SA risk sits with you, the owner is purely taking the risk that your company could stop paying the rent. The landlord will view guaranteed timely rent, no void periods, no utility bills, weekly inspections, no seasonal variation, and a value for money maintenance service as a lower risk than if they accept a regular tenant.

BENEFITS TO YOU

Not having to make a large investment in a property means you have a comparatively low set up cost. I have covered some of the costs involved earlier but the main initial cost is going to be the first month's rent and maybe a deposit but there are ways that you can mitigate even these costs. For example, I took on a R2SA and negotiated to not pay a deposit in exchange for the landlord benefits listed above, and a rent of £600 pcm. The landlord agreed to completely refurbish the property and furnish it as per the SA requirements, at his cost. I quickly listed the property with a corporate provider of short-term guests (I will cover this later) and subsequently I had a booking for £3,500 for a month. I took the keys for the already furnished property on the Friday and I welcomed my guest from overseas on the Sunday.

The main point to understand is that in the worst-case scenario, your costs are going to be the first month's rent, the deposit, and the furniture which you could even hire if you wish. I also have a broker who is able to raise all this relatively small amount of start-up capital for the people who I teach and mentor in SA from crowdfunding websites.

So, people with literally no money can get started in SA, but you will also be avoiding the traditional property acquisition time and cost, which can be extensive. For example, the landlord will have to make an offer on the property, usually via an estate agent and hopefully the offer is accepted without too much delay. Then it's over to the solicitors and unfortunately that's when things seem to take far too long. Sometimes things that should only take 4-6 weeks can drag on for six months and that's even without significant issues to overcome regarding the title, or the searches, or a chain break, or valuations not satisfying lenders to name but some of the regular hold ups. Sometimes the hold-up that you hear from your own solicitor is that "it's with the other side". Unfortunately, this is often code for your file has not found its way to the top of the in tray yet and so I will blame someone else in the meantime and you can wait! I have often called a solicitor's bluff on that excuse and proved, because I know the other solicitor, that it isn't 'with the other side' at all.

Once all this is done, there's the issue of the large lump sum of cash required for the purchase which might be a deposit, or it might be the whole purchase price. Once the sale goes through, there may be some refurbishment to be done to get it ready to let. This process often drags on much longer than the landlord hoped it would due to the builders and tradespeople taking much longer than they promised to do the work and more often than not, needing more money than the original quote to do the work due to unforeseen circumstances.

Finally, the house is ready and the landlord either uses a LA or tries to get a tenant themselves, but this can often take far too long and in the meantime all the bills need to be paid and there is still no money coming in from this property. When the tenant eventually moves in and the haemorrhaging of money finally stops it's time to work out how much is actually coming in. The typical scenario for a mortgaged BTL is that they make circa £150 pcm but they will also get taxed on that. Yes, some will make more but equally some will make less. Many landlords are making a loss each month even with tenants paying rent because the yield margins are so poor.

So, let's say the landlord is making £150 pcm until the tenant moves out and as I mentioned in the earlier section all of their profit is wiped out in between tenants, only to start the whole process all over again! Unfortunately, this is the reality for many BTL landlords, but your strategy will be to provide a much better alternative for them by interrupting this cycle and taking the property as a R2SA.

Blake Bettley – Hygge Homes

" From a young age I have always been interested in finance, business and entrepreneurship. Whilst I started working as an IT contractor at the age of 22, I knew that I wanted more from life than the daily grind. I wanted financial freedom through my own business. A business which is leveraged enough to free up time to spend with my partner, family and friends, as well as travel and enjoy life a bit more! I decided to attend a networking event and was signposted to a property training event where Kevin was speaking about Serviced Accommodation. After a full-on weekend I decided that I wanted to try the R2SA strategy as it didn't require much up-front investment and was a lower risk than some of the other options. I booked onto the Serviced Accommodation Intensive course, and thereafter the Mastermind mentorship both run by Kevin and Caroline. They were so helpful, they set me goals and deadlines to really push me to go out and have a go. I went on to get my first Rent to Serviced Accommodation property in Chester using the techniques and tips that I had learnt. At the time my partner, Jen, was a senior manager in Legal services and was unhappy in her role. This turned out to be great timing for both of us, as she was able to leave her role to grow and run our business, Hygge Homes in Chester, allowing me to continue to contract and provide us with financial security. It is always a risk to start a business, but between us we have different abilities and strengths which complement each other. Whilst you always wonder whether the business model will work in reality, of course it did and we have built a business which is profitable and stable, with strong processes and financial reporting allowing us to track our progress. We now have 7 properties and are continuing to grow and leverage our business. Kevin and Caroline have really changed our lives and helped us to take a step into the unknown and succeed at it. We are always looking for new opportunities and are so grateful to them for helping us to start our business journey.

WHERE TO FIND LANDLORDS

Online Letting Agents

Many landlords these days advertise their properties themselves using online LAs (*Google* it for current ones). On these sites a landlord can upload their own photos and description of the property. Some of the sites offer a viewing service where a local rep will show the prospective tenant around and some require the owner to do the viewing. After the viewing, the Online Agents have a credit referencing service and so once the applicant has passed, the agent will send the tenancy agreement (or the landlord can use his/her own agreement). At this point the prospective tenant is able to communicate directly with the owner/landlord and that's when the SA operator can explain the benefits to them of SA.

My view on this is that the very worst thing that can happen is the owner might say no. Yes, I can understand why people are worried about getting a no, but the more you do it the easier it gets. One of my mottos is that I buy or rent the properties where the answer to my offer is yes, and I don't when the answer is no, and if you make more offers you are more likely to get a yes! So, don't be afraid of a no, just see it as being one step closer to your next yes. If you use your networking skills and build a rapport with the landlord first, then you are more likely to get a yes and remember, practice makes perfect.

Property Networking Meetings

Property networking meetings are a great place to go to meet landlords, *Google* it to find ones in your area. Some are free to attend but typically, at the time of writing, they cost £20 and they usually take place from 7pm - 9pm. If you go regularly you will definitely get to know landlords and you will soon learn that many of them are fed up and even the ones that aren't fed up will be interested with what you can offer them if you rent their property and use it as SA. Remember, no more tenant problems, no voids and the property kept in show home condition.

Business Networking Meetings

Business networking meetings are also a good place to go to find landlords. If you take the Business Network International (BNI) as an example, you are able to view via the respective 'Chapter' website who all of the members of the chapter are and what their profession is. Ideally you should choose a chapter that has property types there. BNI chapter members will very often include an estate agent, a letting agent, an accountant, a solicitor, a mortgage broker, a cleaning company owner, and an insurance broker as well as many trades like builders, electricians and plumbers. A BNI network chapter that I used to be a member of had all of these people as fellow members as well as a multitude of other professions represented.

The concept of business network meetings is that each member is incentivised to help the other members get more business by giving referrals or introductions or advice on each other's business. The phrase 'givers gain' is referred to at every meeting. BNI is a great place to source 'power team' members for your SA business and so you will definitely be able to provide referrals and leads and help them with their business by giving them the opportunity to quote to provide services for you in your business.

At every meeting each member gets a chance to say what they need most help with and you could simply say "I would like introductions to landlords as I would like to rent their property from them on a long term basis whilst keeping them in show home condition". Everyone in the room will be listening and if they can help you, they will. Remember, choose which BNI meeting to join wisely because one of the members is likely to be an estate agent or LA! You can visit several times without actually joining as a full member which will allow you to try it out first to see if it's for you. I would be quick if I were you because when other people who live in your area read this book they might rush down and join their local BNI and there is only one member of each trade or profession allowed per chapter so you will want to take the SA operator slot!

Landlord Meetings

You can also go to landlord meetings, for example those arranged by the local council and the ones I've been to are full of disgruntled landlords challenging and complaining to the council employees about how little help they get from the council and how badly BTL landlords are treated by the government etc. With R2SA you can help relieve a lot of their stress.

Social Media/Self Promotion

I often advise my students to post on their own social media that they are looking to rent property long term where they will guarantee the rent and keep the property in show home condition. The way social media works is that people know people who know people and so very quickly you can be introduced to your next R2SA landlord. You may find that your direct friends list contains someone who would happily trust you with their property. The other tool currently on *Facebook* is marketplace and there is a 'properties to rent' tab where you can also get in direct contact with the landlord. Then there are simply people that you know or meet. If you are always telling people what you do and that you are always looking for property to rent, you are more likely to get R2SAs.

Landlord "Perks"

I have had owners ask if they can still use the property from time to time if there are no bookings, or even have 'mates' rates', but our response is always no as we are paying them a full month's rent. Even if there was no current booking you would need to block the property off to allow the owner to stay and whilst that time is blocked off, you could be missing out on a nice booking from one of the OTAs, but because your property wasn't visible to the person going on to *Booking.com* for example, they booked somewhere else. Remember, many bookings are made in the last two weeks before the check in date.

The other thing to consider is that you will need to send the cleaners in to clean and to replace all of the linen and towels etc. and this will need to be paid for. So, mates' rates wouldn't make you much money and it could cost you by missing out on a lucrative booking. When we explain this to the landlord they always understand, and you can't blame them for asking but you should take this stance too in order to make more money from your business.

Dave and Fliss Lewis –
Red Lanyard Apartments / Red Lanyard Hotels

❝ We attended Kevin Poneskis' training in April 2019 and immediately signed up to the SA Mastermind starting in May. Our story is probably not that different to anyone else reading this book; want to get into property, don't know how, assume you need lots of money first etc. But we have always had a passion for hospitality and nurtured the idea of owning our own hotel, an idea that is now becoming a reality!

Having received expert training from Kevin, Caroline and their team, we knew that if we were to give ourselves a bigger challenge and more ambitious goals, we should join the Mastermind Programme. During this 6 month mentorship we have taken on two R2SA units and are currently securing our first management deal for a 3 bed house.

Our first unit was a 1 bed studio which after the second month earned a £800 net profit which enabled us to take on a VA to help with daily business admin. The second unit was a 3-bed townhouse, this almost immediately attracted a month long booking from a contract firm which earned us a £1200 net profit for the month - and then they extended by another month! This was particularly good considering it was November and December.

The management deal will be our first. This was a friend who had a 3-bed house and wanted to rent it out initially. However, having seen what we were doing with *"Airbnb"* he wanted more income. When we told him about the Capital Allowances and Section 24 benefits he was sold!

But the most exciting part of the journey so far is the JV partnership we formed at the mastermind. We gave ourselves the challenge of acquiring a guest house within the 6 month programme; and we're pleased to say that we are about to exchange contracts on a 10 Bed Grade 2 listed guest house that we will convert to a 14 bed Boutique Hotel. The numbers in the Deal Analyser were eye watering in terms of revenue and profit, not to mention the GDV of the business if we achieve the average daily rate (ADR) and revenue per available room (RevPaR).

And of course, there's the CAs. The report we received from the CA surveyor indicated that we would receive c.£150K in allowances, which means up to £60K tax free income for us and our JV Partners!

We started out as Red Lanyard Apartments and are now adding Red Lanyard Hotels to our brand group. Acquiring and operating SA apartments and houses certainly gave us the insight and knowledge to take on greater challenges. Thanks to the education, mentoring and peer learning from the training and mastermind we have been awarded an overall performance score of 9.8 by *Booking.com*. It has been a very exciting 10 months but also hard, but it's the hard that makes it worth doing!"

#18. R2SA Via a Letting Agent (LA)

At the time of writing, LAs are having restrictions imposed on them to cap the fees that they can charge to prospective tenants. This means that LAs are going to make less money during a void period because firstly, they won't be able to charge their management fee to the landlord on rent received because there isn't any, and secondly, they won't make the same money they previously did from tenant referencing. So, the LA is going to be even more incentivised to have uninterrupted rent coming in from each and every one of the properties on their books. This is where the SA operator comes in to create a win-win scenario by offering to take the property for the long term.

Firstly, you should ask the LA if the landlord would be happy doing a company let on the property. You can position yourself in different ways, some SA operators who do R2SA call themselves an 'Accommodation Company' or a 'Relocation Company', or whatever works or feels best for them. You explain that you will be using the property as SA and that your main focus is providing accommodation for corporate clients as I covered earlier.

Corporate guests should be your main focus because you will be able to get much longer bookings from companies than you will be able to get from leisure guests. If you have done some prior legwork you will be able to name certain companies, and ideally a specific person there, who you have spoken to about offering an alternative to hotels for their visiting employees and clients.

In my opinion you should mention to the LA that you will also be advertising the property on *Booking.com* and *Airbnb* because that is another avenue for getting corporate bookings. This is 100% true as we get countless corporate long stay bookings via these portals because the member of staff whose task it is to find accommodation for the employees or clients of the firm, simply go on to the OTAs in order to do it. They aren't specifically looking for SA, but more and more they are finding and choosing SA because it provides a much better alternative to a hotel and more often than not at a cheaper price, especially when it saves on more than one hotel room.

It is wise to tell the LA that the property will be listed on OTAs otherwise if they or the landlord "discover it" on their own, they may react badly and attempt to cancel the contract. In this situation if you've got lots of forward bookings you may have a significant problem providing alternatives for them. Even if you don't have lots of forward bookings to deal with, the last thing you want to do is have this money-making machine (if done properly) pulled from you prematurely losing any initial investment. You will also have lost the opportunity to make a lot of money compared to a R2SA that has been operated for several years without interruption. The LA or landlord might say no if you mention listing on *Booking.com* and *Airbnb*, but you will have the opportunity to explain the checks and balances of your business to prevent potential problems. I would rather spend all of the time required launching an SA unit without the constant worry that it could be pulled at any moment for being listed on a particular OTA.

The scenario which is a little ironic is that many LAs and landlords will not have an issue with you being listed on *Booking.com* but will not like you being on *Airbnb*. This is because much of the bad publicity out there comes from *Airbnb* bookings where a very naive, or untrained, or reckless person listed their property on *Airbnb* without the proper safeguards in place like credit card details, deposits, checking previous host reviews and not allowing one night stays. Failure to implement these simple steps resulted in a huge party which made the news because of the disruption caused to the neighbours and the surrounding area in general.

One of the reasons these parties happen is because the *Airbnb* host allows a one-night stay at the property. With *Airbnb* you actually have more control over who stays in your property because you can be set to 'enquiries only' which means you can say no to a guest if you have any doubts about them. With *Booking.com* you are automatically 'instant book' which means that if someone books and pays, unless you can prove to *Booking.com* they are a guest who is going to cause problems, they will be coming.

The reality for most areas is that 90% of your bookings will come from *Booking.com* over all of the other OTAs put together and so if you really want it and the only way to get the property is to promise not to list on *Airbnb*, then you should seriously consider it. The bookings that you might have got via *Airbnb* would ultimately have blocked out your calendar and prevent bookings you would have got anyway from *Booking.com* instead. I think in most cases not being on *Airbnb* would not have too much of an impact financially, but if you can have them both then that's clearly better. So, when explaining to the agent why they should support your application for the property, you should make it clear to them that you are looking to take the property on a long-term basis which could easily be several years. We recommend at least a one-year contract and always include a sensible break clause. What the agent will be hearing at this point is long term uninterrupted income.

It's very important that you explain clearly that your company will be liable for the rent. You should repeat this at least once more when it's appropriate because this can be the main sticking point if they didn't register this important point the first time. Often agents will wrongly assume that if you don't get a client in the property the rent won't be paid. If they think that is the case, you won't be getting the keys to the property! The problem is that sometimes when an agent doesn't fully understand your business or what you are proposing they will often just say that the owner does not want to proceed, when the reality is, they misunderstood something fundamental like guaranteed monthly rent. You need to make it clear that they will be referencing and doing the credit check on your company. If applicable, you also need to explain to the agent that you are establishing a brand-new business in the area and you have opened a new Ltd Co. to operate it. For people that I mentor, I am happy to call the agent myself to explain things and I position myself as a colleague, which is true if they are part of my mentoring programme.

Nilanjana Chakraborty –
Niksa Serviced Accommodation

❝❝ If you don't achieve your dreams, someone else will hire you to achieve theirs...

I worked in HR for years. I had a very big salary and I worked long hours, but I was not happy. I was struggling to keep up with my responsibilities as a mother of a 3 years old daughter. Very soon my health started to be affected and also my relationships. So, one day I decided to 'fire my boss' and follow my dreams...my dreams to get back into hospitality where I began my career years ago. I had the passion, the drive, but I didn't know where to start.

I was recommended to attend Kevin's SA course by an ex-colleague who highly rated him. I booked myself in and on his 2 days course, Kevin taught us every step of running an SA business; right from due diligence, how to talk to an estate agent through to setting up and running it. Applying the tools and knowledge provided in the SA course I soon started with two Rent to SA properties and within a year I now have four. My most daunting experience was approaching the local letting agents and convince them on Rent to SA. They quizzed me in detail and asked every possible question on the topic. Thankfully I had Kevin's script in my hand, and it had everything covered. After practising Kevin's script with two local agents I convinced a third one and have been working with them for the past year. They sourced all my SA deals and they keep coming with more.

I won't lie; running this business is a complete rollercoaster. It's thrilling, it's exciting and you may never know what's next. I am extremely fortunate to have Kevin a phone call away and all the other friends I have made. I absolutely love my SA business and will not trade it for anything else. We are *Airbnb* Superhost for the third time in a row and have secured multiple direct bookings which we have converted from our OTA bookings. Now I have flexibility and time to spend with my daughter. I enjoy every moment of watching her grow up.

Hopefully, in the near future I will be able to achieve my dream of owning a chain of aparthotels. And guess who I will be asking for help and advice? Our Property Soldier Kevin Poneskis."

You need to make the new company situation clear because when the external credit reference agency that the agent will probably use to do the referencing does their checks, you brand new Ltd Co. with no turnover is going to fail due to lack of turnover and trading history. Tell them in advance that this is likely to happen so that it doesn't cause any concern but reassure them that you or one of the other directors of the company will stand as the guarantor. The scenario of someone standing as a guarantor for someone (or in this case a company) when it comes to credit checking will be normal for the agent. If you or maybe your business partners are unlikely to pass a credit check then you will probably need to ask someone else to do this for you who will pass.

You won't be bothering the agent every time something minor in the property needs to be fixed like a leaky tap. The reason for this is you don't want to be relying on the agent to get tradesmen out to the property to fix very minor things. If you have got your own trusted and reliable trades or a handyman to do things like this, your business will run smoother. This is because the repair will probably happen quicker, which will keep your guests happier and you will be able to control when the repair happens. You will find it very hard to control when the LA's plumber goes to the property because of the lack of direct communication and if you have guests in place at the time, it would not be ideal if the guests were not expecting someone. Even though this should be music to the LAs ears you might decide not to mention it because they will not want to have repairs taking place by people they do not know, and often the LA will pass on a fee to the landlord for arranging the repair.

The person who should appreciate you the most is the landlord, especially if they are experienced because they will notice that while you have been in the property their average maintenance and repair costs have decreased. The other reason that the LA and landlord will grow to appreciate you is that when the regular inspections take place by the LA the reports will be excellent in terms of how nicely the property is being kept. Most LAs will do these quarterly. If you don't get an excellent score, I would suggest that something drastic is going wrong that you need to address!

These inspections are another reason why you should be clear from the outset on how the property is going to be used because if you've got guests who have booked for say two nights via *Booking.com* and this booking coincides with the inspection the LA would easily find out then. It would be difficult for you to try to get the agent to do the inspection in between your bookings because they will want to do it at a time that's convenient to them not you. They are unlikely to give a specific time for the inspection; it is more likely to be a 'morning' or 'afternoon' slot. The thing to say to your guests when this inspection takes place is that a member of your team will be dropping by at some point (morning or afternoon) to do a routine maintenance inspection so that they are not surprised by the visit. In most cases your guests are going to be out during the day anyway.

Most people are used to hotel staff having access to their rooms and so it will probably not be a problem for them. If however your guest does have an issue with the 'maintenance' inspection because they want total privacy or they are working shifts and so need to sleep when the inspection is due then it will be fine on these occasions to ask the agent to do the inspection at a different time, ideally in between your next check out and check in. The agent will have a certain amount of flexibility especially if you tell them that your client (remember it's best to use the term client to the agent) is working shifts and will be sleeping at the proposed time. This won't be unusual for them because many of their BTL tenants will also need to sleep at unusual times of day.

As you can see there are more moving parts involved when it comes to R2SA via a LA verses R2SA direct to a landlord. In my opinion, people who want to build their R2SA business should try to source their initial properties from a landlord first. The main reason for this is because it's easier to establish credibility with a LA if you already have one or two SAs in the area and your Ltd Co. does have some trading history. Something that works really well is to invite the agent to have a look at your existing SAs. In my experience they never take you up on the offer, but the fact that you offered will reassure them that you are not a 'here today gone tomorrow' business, but an established one that is more likely to pay the rent on time. If the agent does take you up on the offer, it's not like you have to go there and then, so don't worry about that too much. You can simply say "ok fine, I will check with my current clients when would be a convenient time to do it and I will schedule it in" and take it from there.

Many people prefer to go directly to LA instead of landlords because they perceive it as the 'lowest hanging fruit' but I believe the opposite is the case because of all of the extra moving parts that I've listed above. There is no right or wrong and so it's simply a case of each to their own.

Ben Brand – Stay BC

❝ Hi there, my name is Ben Brand and I run a Serviced Accommodation (SA) business in Newport, South Wales called StayBC, along with my business partner Chris Puckett. I first became interested in SA in the spring of 2019 after coming across Kevin Poneskis' excellent Serviced Accommodation Property Podcast. At the time I was just over a year away from the end of my career in the British Army and I was starting to look for a new and exciting career. A big motivation for me was to take on a new challenge that would also allow me to spend more time with my wife and daughter, something that had been difficult in the army. Kevin's story and the information he provided on his podcast really resonated with me, so I decided to attend one of his SA Discovery Days.

I thoroughly enjoyed the Discovery Day and it helped finalise my decision to start my own SA business. I knew that I would significantly improve the chances of my business succeeding by getting trained and mentored by people who had already walked the path I was about to head down. As a result, I decided to book myself on Kevin and Caroline's two day SA Intensive course in July 2019. The training was excellent and at the end of the course, I decided to enrol in their SA Mastermind as I wanted ongoing support, advice, and accountability to help me set up my business.

Following the course my business partner and I chose the city of Newport, South Wales to start our SA business as we believed it was up and coming and started looking for our first Rent to SA in September 2019. Using the training and knowledge I received from Kevin's course and Mastermind, we were able to find our first Rent to SA within a couple of weeks through a letting agent. We were then able to source another three units over the next couple of months bringing us to a total of four units, at the time I am writing this in January 2020. We currently have more Rent to SA deals in the pipeline and are looking for our first purchase property to use as SA. We have also attracted several investors and have bigger projects timetabled for later in 2020 including an SA Apartment Hotel and SA developments in Newport.

My final day in the army is in May 2020. I am delighted to say that I am on target to replace and exceed my army salary by this date thanks to my SA business, meaning I will never need to work for anyone else ever again which is a great feeling.

It is not in any way an overstatement to say that taking Kevin's SA training and Mastermind has completely transformed my life. I now have a level of drive, ambition, and purpose that I never had before. I am truly grateful to Kevin, Caroline and the wider team for completely changing my life for the better and I am truly excited about what the future holds for me and my SA business. 🙸

#19. SA Management

Once an SA operator gains some experience and knowledge from either R2SA or operating their own property as SA, an option to scale the business is to move into SA Management of other people's property. It's similar to R2SA but with some fundamental differences, but you can still use all of your existing systems and team members to do it. There are two main versions of management which are known as 'Full' and 'Cloud based' or 'Bookings Management', but frankly you can set up your business however you like.

Providing Full Management as an Operator

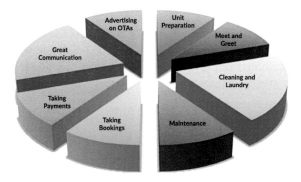

The main difference to running your own property or R2SA is that when you take over management, the owner of the property continues to pay all the bills like the gas, electric and water, but you have the keys and full control of the property. As per the Unit Preparation section later in this book, the property will need to be fully kitted out for SA use.

As the operator you source all the SA bookings via the OTAs, but also from corporate SA companies that I will cover later, as well as direct bookings from your existing clients. The operator charges a management fee which is a percentage of total turnover which in most cases is 15 - 20%. Therefore, £2,500 worth of bookings would generate £500 as your management fee. You will instantly see that you can earn a lot more per property for managing SAs than a LA would get for managing a BTL, but there is obviously more work to do in SA.

It is the operator's role to deduct 'costs of sales' from the booking receipts, which are any costs incurred when taking and fulfilling a booking. So based on the previous example, we have £2,000 in the pot to pay the OTAs their commissions (circa 15%) as well as any other marketing costs. The cleaning and laundry bills, M&G as well as any maintenance costs are also deducted as cost of sales. The remainder is paid to the owner who is responsible for paying all the household bills like a mortgage, and whatever is left is their cash flow. In my experience, the remaining cash flow is usually higher than the equivalent BTL cash flow would have been for the same property. If it isn't it's worth remembering the added value gained through SA, as the manager will be keeping the property in show home condition and the landlord will no longer be experiencing tenant problems that they may previously have had and it will be completely hands free for them apart from continuing to pay direct debits for the bills. They will also be able to avoid Section 24 and claim CAs.

If bills being paid by the owner are a worry or the owner is struggling to keep up with the workload, you or a member of your staff can be added to the account and the utility companies will be allowed to speak to you about anything concerning the account, or you could ask for the bills to be paperless and emailed to you.

When the owner takes responsibility for managing household accounts, you can ask them to provide a photo to demonstrate the bills are up to date and that everything is in order and being paid. It's rare for utility companies to switch things off these days but for peace of mind I would recommend that you know everything is being paid.

Whether you are doing R2SA or Full Management of a property you should make it clear to the owner that they should not go into the property without arranging it with you first, because you will need to ensure there are no guests in residence.

Full Management as an Owner

My advice is that if you are thinking of employing an existing SA company to do full management on your property you confirm that they are fully established in your town or city and they have other SAs in your town or city. This is because it's extremely difficult to fully manage an SA away from your trusted cleaners, trades and handymen and keep everything running smoothly.

If they do have SAs near to you, please ask for the listing details on *Booking. com* and *Airbnb* and take a look at them. If the company has been running for a while there will be enough reviews for you to form an opinion but be aware of fake reviews. It is possible for an operator to get friends, family and employees to leave high scored reviews in order to bring their average up. In my experience if you notice a lot of really good ones and a lot of really bad ones this is an indicator that some of the good ones are fake. The odd bad one is almost inevitable, but a lot of unjustified bad ones is extremely unlikely.

If the reviews are bad or suspicious it's an indicator that the SA company is either not functioning too well if they are set up in your area, or they are attempting to operate too far away from their base and that's why the problems are arising. The reason that this is so important for you is that if a property is not run properly you could get complaints from the neighbours, or the block management company if it's a flat, but crucially it will also significantly impact you financially because a badly run SA will inevitably get less bookings and therefore need to set cheaper prices in order to still attract bookings all of which will diminish turnover. The management company will still take their 20% of turnover at source and all the other cost of sales, and you will get what's left. So, if the turnover is low you may not make a profit and you could even find yourself in a deficit situation.

To avoid a loss making business and to incentivise the operator, I would be very careful with any contract that you sign. I suggest as a bare minimum you have a break clause which states that if the monthly payment to you drops below a certain level or if a pattern of poor performance emerges, then you will be released from the contract. I have heard of people in a deficit situation for long periods and the management company will not release them from the contract, so please don't find yourself in that situation by signing an unfair, one-sided contract.

Charmaine Thomas – De Luxe Short Stays

" I have worked in property for the last 7 years, mainly in BTLs/ Renovations. In March 2019 I decided to attend Kevin's 2 day SA Intensive training, which opened my mind to a new strategy. I then decided to join the 6 month SA Mastermind program to get ongoing help and support. During my first month I was able to get 2 R2SA units & was able to apply my training immediately using the correct tools & systems recommended. I knew I wanted to grow my business significantly and so I set myself a target of 15 properties by the end of 2019.

Lucky enough for me, I have a best friend who was up for a challenge and left her full time employment to help grow De Luxe Short Stays. This was an initial investment from my part which helped me grow the business. I knew we both had different skill sets to complement each other and the company. Sade Cooke, now my partner in De Luxe Short Stays, main role is to Source R2SA units for myself or investors & to build company relations to secure those beautiful long stay corporate bookings. With patience and persistence, we have managed to secure contracts with one of the country's leading producing theatres. Alongside this a major sporting club in Nottingham and Contractors who have been with us since March 2019. We don't just want to provide a stay for our guests, we want to provide that Deluxe feel & build a working relationship for both our guests and the companies we work alongside. Personally, I find the SA strategy not an easy one. But I can honestly say if you are in it for the long game & you have a positive mindset, there are no limits to what you can achieve.

I have a winning mentality and I'm not afraid to work extremely hard and learn plenty of lessons along the way. As long as I am moving forward and reaching personal goals for me & my little girl Lyla, life is good. Myself and Sade have built something special in my hometown of Nottingham, we plan to expand in a few more major cities working alongside some fantastic investors. In 11 months, we have achieved 5 R2SA properties and 10 SA Management. 13 properties have been sourced by ourselves with hard work and building trust with 3 major estate agencies in Nottingham. We are professional and trustworthy, and this is extremely important when working with agents whilst building a reputable business and brand. This journey has provided different income branches which include R2SA, SA Management, & SA Design.

I'm looking forward to what 2020 brings and I would like to thank Kevin and Caroline for their continued support and fabulous friendships made. 〃

Cloud or Bookings Management

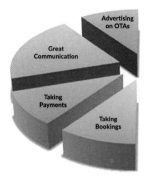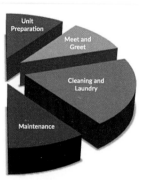

The pie chart shows the roles and responsibilities of the operator on the left, and the owner/landlord on the right when setting up and running an SA property.

The main difference between full management and cloud or bookings management is that with cloud or bookings management you as the operator are only responsible for managing the listings, accepting bookings from OTAs and direct clients, getting terms and conditions signed, taking payment, guest communication prior to them arriving at the property and getting them to the door. The owner is responsible for the customer experience once they have arrived, i.e. property set up, quality of cleaning and linen, responding to maintenance requirements, dealing with any breaches of terms and conditions etc. Essentially the owner looks after the property 'on the ground' and you handle the 'online' activities.

Benefits to the Owner

As the experienced partner you may give advice and help when it comes to putting the right-hand side in place because ideally you have already done it on your own properties or R2SAs. I would suggest that it would be in your best interests to help the owner get this right because it can impact you. If the owner requires a lot of help, for example ordering furniture, you could do this for a setup fee, but It is the owner who pays for all of the furniture and equipment required. The size of this fee would depend on the amount of time/work involved.

The benefit of cloud or bookings management to the owner is immediate access to your established business and connections leading to more bookings directly from companies and the corporate SA companies like Silver Door and Situ. In exchange for immediate access to booking demand, the owner will be paying for example 10% commission to you, but they are saving money and time on not having their own systems in place. Unless they have had some training, they may not know or want to know how to do everything on the left hand side of the chart.

Challenges for the Operator

In my opinion cloud based/bookings management' should not be entered into lightly. As an operator it may seem like a great easy way to earn money by simply plugging someone else's property into your existing systems like the channel manager and channel manager but if the owner is not looking after their side of the arrangement it will cause you hassle. Remember it's not up to you to manage the cleaners but if a guest turns up and the property hasn't been cleaned since the previous guests left you will be dealing with the complaints from the guest and if this is a regular occurrence your listing on the OTAs will be getting a bad review, and if you don't maintain a high review score you will not be able to demand a high nightly rate and you are likely to get less bookings. If you operate under a specific brand across your own, R2SA and managed properties, this could have a negative impact across your business, not just for this specific property. Maintenance is the other main issue that will cause complaints and bad reviews, so the owner needs to be on top of this to keep everything running smoothly. I hear more often than not that this arrangement doesn't work well, which is why I choose not to offer it as I would much rather be in control of my business and not be at the mercy of others.

#20. Buy to Let Conversion

As I have previously stated many people have a perception that SA is fancy waterside apartments and they do not consider that other types of property work perfectly well as SA too. For many years I built up a BTL portfolio and in recent years I've been converting many of these flats and houses into SA. I get a property back from a tenant in one of two ways, either the tenant ends the tenancy as normal, or like many landlords, I must evict.

I evict if the rent is not being paid, or the property is not being cared for properly, or both. Naturally I have sympathy for those who genuinely fall on hard times, but for some I see paying rent coming far down their list of priorities in terms of what they should be spending their money on. I am happy for my good BTL tenants to stay for as long as they remain good tenants.

When I receive a property back, I have to make the decision whether it will work as SA or not. I do this by analysing the suitability of the property and the demand as covered in a previous section. If the answer is no, I sell it and reinvest into properties that do work as SA.

If I do decide to keep the property and there is a mortgage on the property, permission needs to be granted by the lender to allow SA use, and if permission isn't granted the loan can sometimes be replaced with a bespoke SA product. SA specific insurance needs to be put in place (see SA insurance). The property will need to be furnished and fully kitted out with everything needed to provide a 'home from home' for the guests.

Laura Barrell

"" My SA journey started from both a good and a bad position. Yes, I had 3 single let properties, but I had also stupidly sold a flat, reacting to a dire situation following a failed off plan investment, bad mortgages and basically muddling along without a strategy. I was also in a j.o.b. that I was desperate to leave but also permitted no capacity at all for taking phone calls or answering emails in the day as I was in a military medical centre and doing a 3 hour commute.

A friend suggested property training and I was drawn to the SA model as my primary goal was to cash flow myself out of my job. This would buy me the time to progress other strategies and SA seemed a good way to achieve this. After completing the training with Kevin, it must have been fate - a tenant handed in their notice at a house I owned! The house was a 2 bed just outside Bristol. An unremarkable property in a quiet backwater. Taking Kevin's approach, I started with D - Due Diligence. There were several large business parks nearby, but I could find no other units in the vicinity, which was either a good or a bad sign, I decided to take a risk. Using the money from the sold flat, I refurbished the property, furnished it and handed it to an SA Manager. I'd managed to achieve this around my full time job working on a military base. Not easy, every break I had I sneaked away from my desk to the girls changing rooms - the only place my male boss could not track me down. It was a hard time for me, and I became quite ostracised from my colleagues who began to shut me out as I declined all contact during precious breaks. During this time, another tenant handed in their notice. This was a 1 bed flat in the centre of Bristol, and it came with different issues - namely the tenants underneath the flat, also the reason that my tenant was leaving.

By now I was in Kevin's Serviced Accommodation Mastermind group and I took this dilemma to the group. My mentor gave me a strategy that I simply had not seen. He advised that I should approach the downstairs landlord and offer to rent the flat from them if they removed the nightmare tenants from their apartment. To my amazement, she agreed. I was now in possession of the two empty flats which needed furnishing and decorating. My funds were running low and Kevin suggested a furniture finance company during a mentoring call, so I approached one, organising some finance for the new units along with a refinancing of the furniture I'd purchased for the first house. I secured a storage unit and some secondhand furniture from a fellow SA student to finalise all I needed.

So, finally, I had 3 units live and running by the end of my 6 month mastermind programme and I was in the position to hand in my notice to my boss. My strategy had worked, and I'll never forget the feeling of walking away from those colleagues of mine for the last time.

Fig.1.First three months income from each unit
This income is AFTER management fees, cleaning, linen and OTA fees have been deducted. This is my personal gross profit before other bills

	Month 1			Month 2			Month 3		
	Rental income prior	SA income	Uplift	Old BTL rent	SA income	Uplift	Old BTL rent	SA income	Uplift
2 bed house	£ 850.00	£ 2,332.40	£ 1,482.40	£ 850.00	£ 2,166.05	£ 1,316.05	£ 850.00	£ 1,864.83	£ 1,014.83
1 bed flat	£ 850.00	£ 1,546.69	£ 696.69	£ 850.00	£ 1,443.45	£ 593.45	£ 850.00	£ 1,403.62	£ 553.62
1 bed flat (R2R)	£ 895.00	£ 1,287.09	£ 392.09	£ 895.00	£ 1,019.00	£ 124.00	£ 895.00	£ 1,343.00	£ 448.00
Total	£ 2,595.00	£ 5,166.18	£ 2,571.18	£ 2,595.00	£ 4,628.50	£ 2,033.50	£ 2,595.00	£ 4,611.45	£ 2,016.45

Over three months	£ 6,621.13	Over what I would have made renting to tenants & deducting the rental of the R2R
		N.B This profit in these three months theoretically covered the cost of my SA course and Mastermind.

#21. Purchase to SA

I am a great believer in building a property portfolio to provide a financial legacy for ourselves and our loved ones. There will always be a demand for property and so it's a great long-term investment strategy. At the same time as benefiting from capital growth we can create recurring income from property because people are willing to pay us to stay there! The next question to consider therefore, is what is the best income generating strategy for the portfolio?

At present I believe that SA is better than BTL and HMO as it is does not require potentially problematic tenants, provides more income and is eligible for more tax breaks. If these considerations change in the future and a different strategy proves to be better, the good news is that the portfolio can be restructured, or if necessary certain properties could be sold and the money re-invested into more suitable property. The point I am making is that I intend to 'make hay while the sun shines' and make as much money from SA as possible whilst it is the best income generating strategy. For many years I have been operating the 'Buy Refurbish Refinance' model of property investing and using BTL and HMO as the income generating strategy, and now I continue to do the same but with SA.

Over the years I have learnt that the best place to get the highest yield from an investment property like a BTL is to buy one that is in a relatively poor area of town. I don't mean the absolute worst part of town where you wouldn't feel happy leaving your car or where you might not feel physically safe, but not far away. I have found that if you get to know 'your patch' then you can find areas that are ok as 'rentals' as long as you are careful when selecting your tenants.

Careful means doing credit checks, insisting on a guarantor who also passes a credit check and is a homeowner, and asking for previous Landlord references. I have tenants in these areas that have been with me for years and have been no trouble at all. It is inevitable that even if you are careful, if you do BTL for long enough and have multiple properties, you will end up with a bad tenant from time to time, but you just have to take it on the chin.

The main reason to pick these houses to buy is that they have a good purchase price to rent ratio. For example, I have bought properties in South Wales and Devon in the poorer parts of town for £60,000 that I can rent out for £550 per calendar month (pcm). At the time, if I had ventured into a more upmarket area, I might have found a house for £150,000 that I could rent out for £700. The difference in gross yield is significant:

1. £60K property with £550 rent (550x12/60,000x100) = 11% yield

2. £150K property with £700 rent (700x12/150,000x100) = 5.6% yield

The gross yield can be doubled by choosing the poorer areas in which to invest which is the basis on how I built my BTL portfolio. When I first decided to venture into SA, I attended the various courses being delivered at the time and what was being taught is that SA property is mainly smart city centre or waterside apartments. So those are the type of properties I initially sourced in order to do SA. I soon learnt that I was able to make a lot more money from my SA properties than from my BTL ones and so I decided not to acquire any more BTL property, especially as the tax implications were so negative for BTL and so good for SA.

My dilemma came when I got BTL property back from tenants who were moving on. These houses and flats were in the poorer areas of town so surely, they wouldn't work as SA? I decided to give it a try just to see what would happen. I concluded that even if the property wasn't perfect for SA, if it made the same after tax as it did as BTL, I would be happy. I made sure that the property was presented nicely inside with modern furniture so that the photos would look nice for the online portals like *Booking.com* and *Airbnb*, but I also included a photo of the house from the outside so that the guests would not arrive expecting a fancy city centre apartment only to find an ordinary terraced house and leave a bad review. I put single beds in the bedrooms in order to appeal to tradesmen and women predominantly. I hoped that I would attract groups of trades who would choose to save money by staying with us rather than paying for several hotel rooms and hoped that they wouldn't mind staying in a terraced house.

In the very first month of being live with my first terraced ex BTL the bookings came in for that month at just under £2,000 and the profit was just under £1,000. This property continues to return a profit of over £1,000 per month on average. I found that although I only provided single beds, I still got bookings from families as well. So, I would target the trades but accept all comers!

The great thing about appealing to the trades is that as long as you are in a town of over 70,000 people you will have year-round demand, because trades work all year and will need somewhere to stay. It simply means that in the summer you will be able to charge more per night, because the demand will go up through competition form holidaymakers in the summer months. I was very excited, because I realized that I could increase the profit from my existing portfolio by at least five simply by changing them over to SA. As well as the tax benefits that are covered in other sections of this book, the other added benefit was not having the responsibility and worry of having a tenant.

Unfortunately, even if you carefully select a tenant with credit checking and previous landlord references, they can move into your house behaving like Mary Poppins, but later turn into Freddy Krueger. Ok, maybe not that bad but they can trash the property and not pay the rent. The best thing about SA is that it isn't the guest's home, they live somewhere else and are only staying with you temporarily. The guest has paid to stay in advance, you can take a deposit in case of damage and you have their credit card details. It has never happened to me but if a guest refused to leave, I could simply call the police who would remove the guest, just as they would if someone refused to leave a hotel. The guest would not be able to claim tenant rights in a hotel, and the same applies to SA.

Purchase to SA Loophole

I now had a totally new opinion of what property could work as SA and I started to look for more terraced property to buy for SA. The weird thing is that you can even buy property that works great as SA that wouldn't be good enough as BTL and therefore you can get it even cheaper! Let me explain, I bought two houses on one title from an estate agent to use as SA. One of the houses would work fine as BTL, but the other one, which I will call the 'back house', would not because it would not have been a very nice place to live as a permanent residence. The back property had an unusual internal layout in that it is a three-storey house with the kitchen and bathroom on the ground floor, the lounge on the middle floor and the two bedrooms on the top floor. Having no toilet on the top floor would make it annoying to live there full time but luckily, the main bedroom was large enough for me to create a toilet on the top floor and still retain a double room.

The external problems with the back house are that it is quite dark as the windows are close to tall trees which can't be cut down to bring in more light. The only way to get to the back house is to go down some steps which lead to the back of the front house. These steps and the courtyard area leading to the entrance to the back house are also shared with the front house and this will have led to disputes between the previous residents over rubbish, cigarette butts and general arguments that occur when people must share their space with others.

The point I am making here is that I would not have chosen this property to use as a BTL because I would have spotted that these issues would have arisen. I would have had to deal with fighting tenants, and especially in the back house, tenants would be more likely to leave prematurely once they had found a nicer house to live in.

To ease the problem, the rent on the houses would have to be cheaper for tenants to accept compromises, especially in the back house, and the void periods in between tenants would prove to be very expensive and can completely wipe out the modest BTL profits. The fact that these issues would put off owner occupiers as well as investors looking for BTL property means that the value of the houses was significantly impacted. The 'loophole' that I am referring to is that these problems that would put off full time residents of the houses are much less of an issue for short term guests. Your guest will be mainly motivated by saving money on a hotel and so as long as the property is clean and presented nicely inside and their car is safe outside, they will be happy. At the time of writing I have had these houses for over two years and the average review score on *Booking.com* (out of 10) is 9.3.

Refurbish - Refinance SA

I was able to buy the front house and back house, do an extensive refurbishment, and refinance them onto a 70% LTV SA project, pulling all my money out ready to be reinvested! In a nutshell I have ended up with the houses for nothing, because I have got none of my money left in the deal, which makes it an infinite return on investment. The houses qualify as FHL so I can still offset all of the mortgage interest against the income and not be hit by Section 24 tax. Plus, I have claimed thousands of pounds in CAs!

Here is a screenshot of part of the CA report for this house. The plant and machinery in the house created a claim of £63,739. The second screenshot is the land remediation relief (LRR) claim for treating the Japanese knotweed at the house. At the time of writing you can get 150% relief on the cost of treating knotweed. You can also claim this relief for treating asbestos and oil/petrol contamination when doing a refurb project into SA. The cost of treating the knotweed was £3117 x 150% = £4676 which brings total CA claim £68,415 which is 42% of our total expenditure on the project.

Data and Telecommunications Installation	6,023
Electrical - General Lighting	3,385
Electrical - General Power	4,890
Electrical - Power Supplies To Fixed Plant & Machinery	4,492
Electrical - Switchboards & Switchgear	1,505
Fire Alarms, Fire Fighting & Containment	986
Furniture, Fittings and Equipment	1,290
Kitchen & Canteen Fittings	3,129
Mechanical - Cold Water Installation	1,006
Mechanical - Gas Installations	980
Mechanical - Heating Installations	13,700
Mechanical - Hot Water Installations	5,036
Mechanical - Ventilation Installations	1,434
Mechanical Doors, Gates and Shutters	374
Miscellaneous	516
Sanitary Fittings	9,184
Signage	135
Soft Furnishings	5,674
Total Expenditure Qualifying for Plant and Machinery Allowances	**63,739**

Abstraction of Expenditure Qualifying for Relief

	£
Provision of Japanese Knotweed Survey	64
Japanese Knotweed Treatment	2,678
Direct costs associated	375
Total Expenditure Eligible for Land Remediation Relief	**3,117**
Total Claim for Land Remediation Relief (150%)	**4,676**

The figures have been abstracted from the expenditure contained within
the contract between :-

and
Knotweed Support - Invasive Weed Specialists
in accordance with the Finance Act 2001, Schedule 22, Part 1.

The front house and back house, after all costs, average over £3,500 combined profit per calendar month! Just to be clear, that's after all the cleaning and laundry costs and after all the utility bills and mortgage costs are paid. That's over £42,000 profit a year from one property deal and there is plenty of equity left in the property and because of the CAs I can earn £68,415 tax free!

The final part of this loophole I am sharing with you is that a house with knotweed is very hard to buy with a mortgage unless there is a treatment plan with an insurance backed guarantee in place. This will inevitably push the purchase price down which means there is a bargain to be had. If you are going to buy with a mortgage you could fix the purchase price of the property using a purchase option before getting the treatment work done. If you were buying without a mortgage using yours or your investors funds, you would simply need to get the treatment done during the refurb so that when you later apply for a mortgage on the property, the lender will be happy if the surveyor identifies the knotweed. I strongly advise that you check with the lender in advance before paying for the survey that they would be happy lending with a treatment plan in place. You should also check the guarantee that the knotweed removal contractor will be able to provide to you and check with the lender whether that guarantee is acceptable to them. I have fallen foul of this in the past which caused a delay getting a mortgage because I had to instruct a different knotweed contractor to re-treat a site because the first contractor's insurance cover was not adequate.

Ultimately with this knowledge you can acquire with confidence property affected by knotweed which would scare off most investors. This means you will be able to get knotweed property really cheap. The icing on the cake is that you will be able to claim 150% of the cost of treating the knotweed if you subsequently use the house for SA. Most of your competitors, who are not doing SA (or doing SA but don't know this loophole) will not be factoring all of these financial benefits into their numbers when evaluating the deal, which will give you a significant advantage.

I often say to people who attend my seminars "how many of these would you need to not have to rely on a job anymore and be financially independent?"

If they say "two", I say "well learn how to do this and go and do it twice!" Yes it might cost some money to attend a quality course that will give you the tools to be able to go and do it, but just think how life changing it would be for you when you can create cash generating machines like the one I have just highlighted. When people say to me that property training courses are expensive, I reply that "ignorance is more expensive!" Ignorance can cause you to work for the rest of your life exchanging time for money and hoping to be able to retire on a pension that is adequate enough to give you a decent standard of retirement. Unfortunately, the fact is that there is no such thing as job security and there is no such thing as pension security either! The money I spent on my education means I will never need a job ever again and my portfolio of property will provide for my retirement and be a legacy to leave for my family.

If I had decided to use the houses as BTL I would probably have been able to get about £350 per month profit whilst rented out, but as I previously stated the void periods would have wiped out the profit as well as having to deal with the inevitable tenant disputes. Even at a suppressed purchase price it would not have been a good investment as BTL, but as SA it works brilliantly.

Pre-Refurbishment Pictures

Post Refurbishment Pictures

Based on this example, you may now be looking at investment property completely differently, and you can exploit this loophole in your town too. Don't fall into the trap of thinking that everyone will cotton on to this and that will drive the prices up, because in my experience "when all is said and done, a lot more is said than done." As far as I am aware, I am the only trainer in the UK teaching this loophole, so provided you don't wait too long you should be able to snap up some really cheap property in your town that doesn't appeal to the masses but works great for SA. Check out my website www.propertysoldier.co.uk to see if you can get on one of my training courses as I often offer some courses for free.

PURCHASE FUNDING

Bank Finance

Banks offer a wide range of products depending on the type of property being bought. The applicant's personal circumstances will also have a bearing on what product or products the bank will offer. My advice is to speak to an experienced independent finance or mortgage broker who will be able to source the best and most suitable product for you.

Interest Only v Repayment Loan

There is no right or wrong in my opinion. You may only be offered one or the other but if you can choose it comes down to what scenario suits you best at the time. An interest only loan unsurprisingly means that you are only paying the interest and not paying off any of the capital. This scenario works well for people who need to create as much cash flow as possible to be able to replace a job income and go full time into property. Many people are frightened of interest only loans, but they are perfectly sound when it comes to investment properties and there are several reasons why.

In my opinion property value will continue to rise in the UK much steeper than the rate of inflation. The reason is that the demand for UK property will continue to grow for the foreseeable future because the population is growing faster than the rate of new housing stock being built. Simple economics dictate that when there is more demand for something, the value of that thing will rise, in this case property. Therefore, when it comes to the point at which an interest only mortgage has to be paid off it is extremely likely that the property the mortgage is secured against will be worth significantly more than the outstanding mortgage. This leaves two 'exit strategies' in that you can either sell the property, or you could refinance or re-mortgage the property in order to pay off the existing loan.

Repayment Loan

Your personal circumstances will dictate the time frame over which the loan has to be repaid. During the course of the loan the monthly payment required will reflect the amount necessary to pay off the debt as well as pay the rate of interest being charged. The monthly payment amount will therefore be higher than that for an interest only loan. The cash flow from the property is clearly going to be less because of this, but the benefit is that the debt will be paid off over the term of the loan.

Cash – Yours or Other People's

Many people are of the opinion that you should never use your own money for property investing. I agree with this to a degree, but If you have a significant amount of your own cash in the bank, in my opinion it is ok to use it when interest rates are low, otherwise it will be depreciating in value sitting in the bank due to inflation.

By investing in property, you can also multiply that money significantly if you know what you are doing. I think it is wise not to invest all of it because that will leave you an amount in the bank which will act as a safety net or buffer, which in my opinion has benefits that outweigh the net depreciation. These days, I try to keep a significant amount as a reserve which is always there to act as proof of funds. Often banks will ask to see how much of your own money you have to act as a deposit before they will give you a mortgage.

Many banks require your deposit money to have been in your bank account for several months, which shows that it has not just 'parachuted in' because you have just borrowed the deposit funds, as banks need to be confident that you will be able to service the loan repayments and not be overstretched by also paying back a loan for the deposit. They want you to have 'skin in the game'. The reality is that the same pot of cash can represent multiple deposits of the same value if you are indeed borrowing the deposit funds from private or angel investors. Another benefit is that if one of your private investors has an emergency and would like their money back before the loan agreement contract dictates, you have the ability to give it back without too much trouble if you decide to do so. This buffer is also a safety net for you in case anything unforeseen happens, like a family emergency that requires funds at short notice.

Most people do not have a lot of their own money to invest and that's where other people's money comes in, but usually people have a mental block when it comes to the concept of raising money from others. People's self-limiting belief is 'why would anyone lend me money' and 'I don't know anyone with money'! I have found that when you can offer someone a better rate of return than they are able to get in the bank (that beats inflation) that's when they will lend you their money. Some people have surprised me over the years when they have told me they have a decent amount of money to invest when my perception was that they wouldn't have much money, and I hear the same from people who I train and mentor. Most people will not advertise that they have money in the bank to friends and relatives because they know that certain friends and relatives will become very friendly all of a sudden!

If you simply let people know what you are doing by word of mouth or social media, and that you use people's money to invest in property giving them a much better rate of return than they can get in the bank, then what you will find is that people will come to you with their money and not the other way around.

Lease Options

There are many things you can lease, usually for a monthly fee, to use for the duration of the lease contract, such as cars and aeroplanes, but without the need to buy them first and you can do the same with property. With purchase lease options, or 'lease options' for short, you can also negotiate a purchase price for the property that gives you the right to buy it at that price during the term of the lease option period. The purchase price negotiated does not have to be set at today's market value, it could be more or less as it simply depends on the situation and what works best for both parties. Often the purchase option price is set higher than today's value to allow for market appreciation, but I reiterate it doesn't have to be higher. I have bought property years after securing a purchase option at a price that reflected the property's value at the time of the option, and yes it had appreciated in value significantly during the option period.

The option period can be virtually any length of time you and the current owner chooses.

The following example explains what a lease option could look like. A property at today's market value is worth £200,000. If the owner was to rent the property out on the open market to a normal tenant on an AST, he or she could get £800 pcm. You as the investor/buyer could take the property on a lease for five years (the option period) and agree to pay the owner £800 pcm during that time. You would have the right to buy the property at any time during the option period for £200,000 and as soon as you have bought the property you would stop paying the £800 per month. At the time of purchase the property could be worth considerably more than £200,000 but you would still have the right to buy it for £200,000.

You will need two solicitors to arrange the lease option and as with any conveyancing process, one will represent the buyer (you) and one will represent the seller. I strongly advise that you use solicitors who are familiar and experienced with lease options because most conveyancing solicitors are not and if everything is not done properly, it could cause big problems from the outset, or at a later date.

Once the contract has been agreed by both parties a restriction is placed against the title of the property which will secure your right to buy it at the agreed price at any time during the option period and will prevent the owner from pulling out of the deal without your consent. Let's say four years into the option period, due to market appreciation, the property had gone up in value by £40,000, the owner would not be able to pull out of the contract so long as you are not in breach of the terms of the contract. You would still have the right to buy the property for £200,000 and you will have that right up to the five-year point. It is therefore very important that you don't leave it too late to exercise your option to buy the property, so I suggest doing this at least six months before the expiry of the option period to allow for any unforeseen delays.

This type of option is great because whilst you have the right to buy the property at the price agreed during the option period, you do not have the obligation to buy it. If at any point during the option period, you decide to give the property back you are within your rights to do so. This would be acceptable as long as you handed the property back in as good, if not in better condition than you received it. Conditions like this would usually be drawn up from the outset by the solicitors. You might decide not to exercise your option to buy if the market has depreciated and it is worth less than £200,000. As long as it is done from the outset you can have a clause that allows for an extension to the option period depending on certain circumstances. One circumstance could be that the market value has dropped and both parties need longer to allow for it to go back up. You can also make an option agreement 'assignable' which means that you could sell the right to buy the property to another property investor. The price you charge the investor would depend on the equity in the deal and the cash flow generated from it.

Options are relatively simple to do when there is no charge against the property which is usually in the form of a mortgage. Most mortgages are either BTL or residential owner-occupier products. The lender's permission would need to be sought if you intended to do SA in the property otherwise the owner could be breaching the terms and conditions of the mortgage. This would also be true for changing the use of a property to an HMO which I have done in the past. If the lender does not consent to SA at the property, then the only other alternative would be to swap to a mortgage product that allows SA. This may not be possible due to the owner's circumstances but worth checking with a good broker to find out.

If you are able to do SA in the property which has a mortgage, remember that the mortgage will still be in the name of the owner and you need to make sure that the monthly mortgage payment is being made. My advice is not to trust the owner to pay each and every month, even if you know them well because that would be too risky in my opinion. In the past I have arranged 'power of attorney' via my solicitor over the mortgage, which gave me control to ensure that the payments were being made to the lender.

Many people question 'why would an owner agree to an option' but the reality is there are many circumstances that would make an option agreeable to an owner. If an owner is in negative equity (the outstanding mortgage balance is more than the house is worth) it would work perfectly. Many people are in this situation because they bought property at inflated prices at the height of the market in 2007/2008. At this time, lenders were offering 110% mortgages which meant that someone could buy something for say £100K with a 110% interest only mortgage and so they could still owe £110K today. The problem is that the property value may have dropped further, or the property today may only be worth £105K and so the owner can't sell it unless he or she can pay from their own funds to make up the deficit so that the lender gets their £110K back.

We have a R2SA property that the owner tried to sell but couldn't because of negative equity. He was using it as a BTL but even fully let out, he was losing money each month because of the mortgage and LA fees. When he was between tenants it was really costing him money because during voids period not only is there no rent, but the owner must pay all the bills as well. Now as a R2SA we are able to pay him more than the max BTL rent and he does not suffer any voids. When the time is right, we will exercise our option to buy the property which will release him from the problem once and for all.

Another reason that people will allow a property to be sold via a lease option is when they have tenant problems. I secured the option to buy a property that was 'unencumbered' which means that it had no mortgage on it and the main reason the owners were willing to do it was because they had 'tenants from hell' and didn't know how to get rid of them.

If someone has an investment property with bad tenants, they are more likely to be 'motivated sellers' which will always create the potential for a 'win-win' situation for both seller and buyer. The vendor may have previously tried to sell but the bad tenants have made that hard due to a lack of cooperation, or due to the state of the property. Either way this is usually very off putting to a potential buyer who does not know how to use the system to evict such tenants, if they were to buy with 'tenants in situ'. The other issue for a prospective buyer is that most lenders (banks) require 'vacant possession' making it impossible for them to buy with a mortgage which is how most people fund their property acquisition. You, as the buyer with property investment training, can take control (not buy yet) of the property with the intention of buying it, with the existing (bad tenants) in situ. It will be your responsibility to evict the bad tenants using the proper legal channels.

Once the option was signed and the restriction placed against the title, I took control of the property, including the tenants. As far as the tenants were concerned, I had just become their landlord and I subsequently served notice requiring possession of the property. I always find it beneficial to have a discussion if possible, with the tenants, to explain the situation clearly, and I was able to do that in this case. I explained that I need possession of the property to rent it out, in order to provide income for myself and my family. I find that tenants are more reasonable with a new landlord, as the 'bad blood' that may have existed with the old landlord will no longer be an issue. I explained to the tenants that if they do not go after the notice period that I will have to apply to the court for possession and if necessary, pursue a County Court Judgement (CCJ) against them in order to recoup my losses. If the tenant doesn't know what the implications are of a CCJ I explain that it will significantly affect their ability to get credit and probably stop them passing a credit check in order to get another tenancy. I do this in a nice but firm way so that they can tell that they are not dealing with a 'pushover' anymore. This usually does the trick and it did in this case and so the tenants left after the notice period. I have had to evict tenants through the courts before and subsequently had bailiffs gain possession which can take several months but ultimately, I have always been able to get a property back sooner or later. The property was in really poor condition so when I took control (with the lease option) I proceeded to completely renovate it to maximise its potential value. I needed £25,000 for the refurbishment work and for bills and general running costs. I borrowed the £25,000 from private investors paying them 8% return on their money for the duration of the loan.

Once the refurb was complete, I exercised my option to buy it and paid £185,000 cash which I borrowed from private investors at 12% interest. The higher interest rate reflected the fact that I only needed the money for a relatively short period of time which was 6 weeks.

The £185,000 was paid into the vendor's bank account via the conveyancing solicitors.

I refinanced the property with a commercial loan in order to pull out enough equity to repay the loans with interest. The new lender's surveyor valued the property at £375,000 which put circa £240,000 into my bank account. This gave me more than enough money to pay the investors back their £185,000 and £25,000 with interest and left a tidy lump sum for me use for future property investing. It's worth pointing out that this lump sum is tax free money because it is borrowed money and interest will need to be paid on it. The income from this and other investment properties pays that ongoing interest. Many lenders will not allow a new mortgage or loan to be raised against a property within six months of purchase or refinance, insisting on the 'six-month rule'. There are certain lenders however who do not insist on the six-month rule especially to more experienced Landlords/ property investors. Speak to an experienced broker to see whether your circumstances would qualify you to get a mortgage from these specialist lenders who will waive the six-month rule.

There are many other ways to structure a lease option to create a win-win situation for buyers and sellers alike. Lease options can solve the puzzle of how to structure a deal but if you cannot figure it out yourself you should consider speaking to a property investor who is experienced in using lease options or an experienced solicitor who may also be able to offer advice.

So, you can see that you can create win-win situations for sellers of property using lease options, which means there are plenty of potential deals out there for you to go and get for yourself!

Vendor Finance

One of the most amazing things I have learnt as a property investor is that a seller of a property is able to pretty much finance your purchase of their property, and yes you did read that correctly! Most people's belief is that money, or the lack of money, is the main stumbling block for someone to build a portfolio of property, but I know that a lack of property investment knowledge is the main stumbling block. I call this knowledge the 'tools in the toolbox' that a trained property investor has in their toolbox of knowledge.

You may be wondering how and why someone would help fund your purchase of their property and the good news is that there are several reasons. One important reason I have found is that the vendor has no immediate plans for the capital they will receive when the sale goes through and so you can provide them with a much better rate of return than they will get in the bank!

If someone were to sell a property in the conventional way and their intent was to put the money released from the sale in the bank, the interest rate they will receive will be very low. Usually the rate of inflation will cause money to depreciate in value whilst in the bank, incentivising investors and property sellers to prefer an alternative solution that will provide a much better rate of return.

You could arrange a vendor finance solution for you to buy their property, but with the released funds, give them a higher return once the property is in your hands. Effectively they will be loaning you back a sum of money post completion which could be up to 100% of the sale price or even more if they have other funds to use!

I have only ever used a private loan agreement between myself and the vendor, but If you are going to use a solicitor to create this contract, or to put a charge against an asset of yours as security, then you will probably need to use different solicitors to do this other than the ones used to do the conveyancing. This is because it may represent a conflict of interest for conveyancers and the bank, if mortgages are involved on either side. If you tell the conveyancing solicitors about the Vendor Finance arrangement, they might be duty bound to inform the lenders how the deal is being structured which might cause the lenders to be concerned and jeopardise the deal. You should answer truthfully all questions asked by the bank, but I see no need to divulge information that has not been asked for.

There is simply nothing wrong with a person lending money to another on a straight loan, and once you have structured a way to buy someone's property, you and the vendor are perfectly entitled to enter into an agreement whereby they lend you a sum of money which you give an agreed rate of return on. In a nutshell this describes Vendor Finance and you can do this with any type of property.

Typically, you would use vendor finance to cut the cost of borrowing, use third party money to do the deal, and raise money more easily as the Vendor is likely to have relatively light lending conditions in comparison to a bank. The money can be used for things like paying back existing more expensive loans, paying back a deposit you introduced from your own capital, or cash flowing the renovations and SA set up for your new business. In the past I have used vendor finance with BTL and HMO property, but I now do it with SA as that makes me more recurring income. More money, less tax and no tenants!

Exactly how the deal is structured varies depending on the situation, but here is an example of how I have used this in purchasing property. The vendor was trying to sell an unencumbered (no mortgage) house but was struggling to do so due to bad tenants. We agreed on a purchase price of £180K for the badly run-down property. I raised the deposit and borrowed the remainder of the purchase amount from a commercial lender and once the initial purchase had gone through and the £180K landed in the vendor's bank account, they immediately loaned back £70K to cover my deposit and the refurbishment. I only had to borrow the deposit funds from private investors for the period between exchange and the loan coming from the vendor. I paid the vendor 8% interest on their £70K for the duration of the loan and once the refurbishment was complete, I refinanced the property with the same commercial lender and repaid the £70K to the vendor. I didn't use my own money, I didn't need to leave money in the property, the lending terms were favourable from the vendor, I was easily able to cash flow the renovation and best of all, the vendor was happy to receive 8% on their loaned funds.

Pension Funding

Using a Pension Fund is a great way to provide finance for property investing. You should always seek the advice of an Independent Financial Advisor (IFA) in order to do this because everyone's circumstances are different, but here are some general points to note. At the time of writing, if you have a pension, or even more than one pension you can ask the Pension Administrator for a transfer value which will give you the sum of money from your pension(s) that could be moved into a Self Invested Personal Pension (SIPP) or a Small Self Administered Scheme (SASS). A SIPP is for one person only but a SSAS can be for up to 12 people to transfer their pensions into. Both can buy commercial property, and both can borrow up to 50% of their value in the form of a mortgage.

A SSAS can lend money to a company if the money is paid back within a reasonable time with interest that reflects a reasonable rate of return (seek current IFA advice). And so, you could lend money to a Ltd Co. that uses the money to do a 'buy refurbish refinance' deal, with the money post refinance being paid back to the SSAS with interest. The SSAS will be left financially better off and the Ltd Co will now own an investment property. If there is not enough money in the deal to generate enough return to repay the SSAS post refinance, then the property could be sold on to generate the required funds leaving what's left as profit.

If the SIPP/SSAS buys commercial property it will benefit from the income generated and the capital appreciation of the property over time. If it meets the necessary criteria (seek IFA advice) that commercial property could be a hotel that you convert into an Aparthotel. In this circumstance you could have 'turbo charged' your (and others') pension that had previously 'flatlined' in terms of growth and return. Also, you could run the hotel using your SA management company, charging a reasonable management Fee, and so providing an income for you at the same time!

#22. Guest House B&B Conversion

One of the most exciting acquisition strategies right now in SA is developing an existing guest house or B&B into what can be referred to as an Aparthotel or Self-Catering Hotel among other descriptions. For this section I will just use the terms guest house and Aparthotel to avoid being too repetitive. This area of SA is gaining momentum since there is an opportunity to significantly increase the earning capacity of the existing business. More and more, people are choosing to stay in self-catering apartments rather than hotels these days, so why not convert a guest house into studio apartments or rooms.

Refurbishment

Conversion is made easier if the existing rooms are already en-suite and if it is possible to insert a small kitchenette into the room to make it a studio. Once a small kitchenette has been inserted into a room, it is no longer necessary to provide breakfast or with some guest houses, lunch and dinner. After all, if your guest has deliberately chosen to book a self-catering studio apartment/room, they will not expect to be fed! If all of the guest accommodation in the building is studios, then there is no longer a need for the large kitchen, dining room, sitting room and in many cases extensive owner's accommodation. This creates an opportunity to convert this space into more studios. We look for the ability to increase the available guest accommodation by 50%.

Ideally when doing a conversion like this you would be able to completely refurbish the whole property which will create several benefits. The property will be a much nicer place to stay in for guests, which will significantly increase the night rate people are willing to pay. Once upgraded the property will be able to cope with the extra hot/cold water, gas and electric demand. The property will be future proofed and require a lot less ongoing maintenance which is disruptive and causes problems for guests and operators alike which in turn is expensive for the operator. The property can be better sound proofed and made energy efficient which saves money and makes for happier guests! Up to date technology can be introduced into the studios such as high speed WIFI and convenient plug sockets and phone charging ports.

Regarding the en-suites, my advice is to steer away from macerating or Saniflo type toilets because these types of toilet are easily blocked by guests who are sometimes not sensible in terms of what they attempt to flush. A macerating toilet will churn up the waste before it moves into the soil pipe. The soil pipe is a lot smaller than a normal toilet soil pipe which is why macerating toilets are used because often there is not enough space or an adequate 'run' for a normal soil pipe to be used. Sometimes too much tissue or wet wipes will block or damage a macerating toilet never mind things that should never be flushed down a toilet that unfortunately some guests will inevitably do. If the property already uses these types of toilet you should seriously consider putting normal toilets in. Sometimes it is possible to create the space necessary to run the soil pipe out by dropping the ceiling below the room in question. As with all renovations of this type the alterations should be done in strict compliance with Building Regulations.

To ensure regulations are adhered to, you can either use the building control surveyor who works for your local council, or you can appoint a private surveyor. Most council surveyors are good and ok to work with but sometimes it is easier to work with a private one. You could get some advice on this from other property developers in your area who will have experience of the council's surveyors and might be able to recommend a private one especially for larger projects.

Finance

The economies of scale with this model are significant in that you can have for example 15 studios all in one building, not scattered all over the city. The uplift in value of the property will then be significant. Commercial property like this can be valued on its Earnings Before Interest, Tax, Depreciation and Amortization (EBITDA) position. In layman's terms its commercial value as a business and not just the bricks and mortar value of the property.

Once a lender is happy with an established higher turnover and profit of the business as demonstrated by its published accounts, the lender will lend proportionately against the uplift in business value. This can create a situation where the property developer can get a significant proportion of his or her investment back out of the deal whilst still retaining a high cash flowing property business. The projections on our current guest house conversion will pull all our purchase and refurbishment cost out of the deal upon refinancing. This represents a massive opportunity to use investor's funds to finance this type of project because it is possible to recycle most if not all their funds on refinance. Alternatively, investors' money could be left securely in the property so the investor could continue to enjoy a very good rate of return on their money.

Ideally the property will already have C1 use class and not need a 'change of use' planning application. You will need to consult with your local planning authority on the refurbishment to ensure that both planning and building control are happy with the alterations to the property. I find it beneficial to use an architect who is used to working with local builders, town planners and building control surveyors. The architect can also advise you on how to maximise the space available and work with you builder and possibly a quantity surveyor to estimate the materials, time and labour costs, which together will form the build cost of the project.

The build cost calculation will be necessary to give to a prospective lender or bank, if you require development finance for the project. You should be aware that when purchasing such a business it is relatively straight-forward for a surveyor to value the property in its existing state as an operating guest house. A survey will always be necessary when buying with bank finance, but you should also always get a survey done even if you are buying for cash (as with any property purchase), otherwise you may find significant issues with the property that are only discovered after the purchase.

The problem surveyors do find with this type of development is projecting what the property's value will be post refurb and once trading, because most have no experience with this type of project. This can hold up your initial bank funds if the surveyor is insisting that your projected figures are wrong. We are currently providing evidence of the capital uplift on a different guest house conversion in order to convince the surveyor that our projections are realistic. Down valuations by surveyors are a pain for all property developers and it's simply a hurdle that needs to be overcome. Once you can show a lender (and their appointed surveyor) the new trading figures for the business when you are established, you will be able to raise funds more easily because you have evidence.

Planning Use Class

You will also find that many properties being used as a guest house still have the C3 use class. In most instances it is the case that 'grandfather rights,' or 'pre-existing use rights', or 'lawful development rights' have been granted by the local authority to allow the business to continue operating instead of insisting on a change of use in order to continue. This is usually because it is the case that the property has been operating as a business for ten years plus and the local authorities have taken a pragmatic approach to allow them to continue even though permission was not actually granted when the owners actually changed the material use of the property.

In order to lawfully operate the owner and/or operator would still need to be compliant with building regulations and fire safety law and have a licence to provide things such as food and alcohol to guests. If you are acquiring a property (remember this might be using a lease option in order to purchase at a later date) you should ensure that the local authority issue a 'Lawful Development Certificate'. You will need your conveyancing solicitor to arrange with the seller's solicitor to apply for the certificate on behalf of the seller if the certificate has not already been obtained.

I strongly advise that you use a conveyancing solicitor who is experienced in this field because a regular one who mainly deals in C3 property will not have the necessary knowledge to represent you properly. This is likely to cost more in legal fees, but in my opinion, it is money well spent, and not an area where you should look to save money. If you find a guest house for sale which is still in the C3 use class, you should be very careful that you do not assume that ten years have passed and therefore a certificate of lawful use can be obtained. We viewed a guest house recently that was on the market for sale as a business, but the owners had only converted it into a business about two years earlier without any permission. The property was non-compliant with fire and building regulations and didn't have fire doors on the bedrooms.

Tax

Regarding CA it's very important to get a CA survey done in advance of exchange of contracts on the property, or at least ensure that the contract clearly states that the CAs are being transferred to you. The CA surveyor can provide you with a '198 Election' which the seller needs to agree on to effectively 'gift' you the CAs that you are acquiring upon purchase of the property. You should ensure that your CA surveyor, property accountant and conveyancing solicitor are all on the same page here otherwise you might lose a significant amount of CAs which could cause you to pay too much tax on your annual profits when running the business.

You will find that the seller's accountant and solicitor often do not understand this level of detail associated with CAs and they will need to be reassured that in most instances it has no bearing on the seller's future tax position, but it will simply help you with your future tax liability. If the seller was going to continue to run a different guest house business, then they might not be willing to allow you to claim the CAs because they would potentially be able to offset them against future income from their new business. In most cases however, the seller will not be continuing in that particular trade and once reassured, will be happy to allow you to claim the CAs that they didn't.

How to Identify a Deal

You can find guest houses for sale with commercial property agents as well as online sites like *RightMove* Commercial. Most properties for sale will not have a for sale sign up because potential guests can be put off from booking because of it. I find that even though a property is not officially for sale the owners would be willing to sell if they were made a respectable offer. I once knocked on four guest house doors and told the owners that I was looking to buy a guest house in the area and asked them if they knew anyone willing to sell. I was invited in and viewed all four, even in the owners' accommodation!

Many of these owners would like to sell if they could, but they find themselves in a difficult situation. Some owners operate their businesses in such a way that they stay below the VAT threshold, which is currently £85,000 of turnover per annum, or even not declare all of their income to HMRC even though the actual turnover of the business is much higher. Unfortunately, in both cases the commercial value of the property/business is suppressed, because a business is valued largely on its turnover and profit. For someone to buy the property with a commercial loan, which is usually the case, the lender, with the help of a commercial surveyor will use the declared accounts to arrive at the property's value. A lender will usually have a maximum loan to value (LTV) that they will permit and currently that threshold for most lenders is 70% LTV. However, the lender will only lend 70% of the value if the declared turnover and profit of the business will support the monthly payments to service the loan. This is called the 'debt service coverage ratio'.

Insufficient headroom in the debt service coverage ratio causes many sales to fall through because people cannot raise the necessary funds to meet the agreed purchase price. Often a seller will have a loan to clear on the property upon the sale, but also, they usually need a certain sum of money from the sale to buy their next property to live in. Remember most guest house owners live in the property and so they need a significant sum of money to fund the purchase of their next home. Often these people are at retirement age and so will struggle to get a residential mortgage due to their age, especially if they are no longer going to be working and earning an income. The catch 22 situation is that they have to sell above a certain price to be able to move on with their lives, but most buyers can't meet that purchase price due to the commercial value of the business they are selling. To top it all off, many other potential buyers who would like to buy the property to live solely as a primary residence, but usually cannot do so with a residential mortgage because of the C1 use class and their intended use of the property.

These circumstances have created a situation where many guest house owners cannot find a buyer at the right price. Buyers either have to be cash buyers and not need a mortgage or they need a significant deposit due to the bank's LTV figure. As with any property purchase a cash buyer is always in a strong position to negotiate a good price, especially if the seller is 'motivated' to move on and doesn't need too high a sum to clear any debt or charge against the property or to buy their next home. These circumstances could make the possibility of a lease option very favourable and can be a very cost-effective way of funding the deal.

I have learnt over the years that timing is the key to creating the best financial outcome when using this method of acquisition and subsequent purchase. Since a commercial property is valued on its EBITDA you will only be able to fully realise its commercial value once you have been trading at maximum potential for the required number of years a commercial lender needs to see to give it this value. This may well be once two years of trading accounts have been provided. You can get paid advice in advance from a commercial surveyor on what an Aparthotel might be worth based on some projected figures to ensure the deal will be profitable, and that you can refinance and withdraw your investment ready for the next deal.

Due Diligence

We use a specific Aparthotel deal analyser in order to create the projection for a surveyor and it requires all the costs of running such a business to be entered which is vital for you and the surveyor to be able to arrive at a projected value. You will need to provide supporting evidence to validate your projections such as night and occupancy rates achievable as well as running costs. A lot of experience and knowledge has gone into creating our Aparthotel deal analyser but at the end of the day it is still a spreadsheet and if you put 'rubbish' in, you will get "rubbish' out, and so if you are even considering doing this type of deal you should definitely invest in some appropriate training and guidance. This form of property investing can be very profitable if done right, but by not investing in the right education, if done wrong, it can prove to be a very expensive one.

Let's say you want to turn a ten bed guest house into fifteen studios, and you project 70% occupancy of each room at the night rate that studio apartments achieve as SA in the area. Once you have done your due diligence on what the property is likely to be worth when refurbished and trading, you can work backwards, or reverse engineer, using the analyser to give you the necessary offer/purchase price that will make the deal stack. I often say to people attending my training courses that you offer what the deal analyser tells you to offer and you buy the houses when the answer to your offer is yes!

It is possible to get a property commercially valued before you buy it at the agreed option price, and I recommend that you do not tell the surveyor if asked what your agreed purchase price is. If asked just say that you are still in negotiation with the vendor. Yes it's a little 'white' lie but unfortunately there's no polite way of saying to a valuer that you just want him or her to simply do their job and value the property based on what it's worth, and not be distracted by what you will be buying the property for which will be a lot less than its current commercial value.

How to Do the Deal

The first time I did this was a real game changer for me as a property investor and made it possible to make a lot of money in property, but to make it work you must do things in a certain order. It is important that you tell the lender that you intend to use this valuation report to apply for a loan with them after you have initially purchased the property (at the option price). It is critically important that you use a commercial surveyor who is on the recognised panel for the lender that you intend to use for your ongoing loan. The bank will give you the list and ask you to choose one from it. Your broker should be able to point you in the direction of a suitable lender who has the necessary mortgage product that you will need at a competitive interest rate.

You don't always need a broker to work with commercial banks, but unless you have a lot of experience in this area it's probably best to use a broker who might earn his or her fee by finding you a better/cheaper mortgage product than you could yourself. Another important step is to ask the lender for a 'decision in principle' (DIP) for a loan based on the current trading accounts you provide and the survey report. If the bank gives you a DIP, then they will have credit checked you or your company or buying entity and it should be relatively straight-forward to go from DIP to actual loan. A successful DIP will give you the confidence to proceed and to exercise your option to buy the property at that stage.

If you don't get a DIP, it could be due to an issue that simply needs to be rectified but may take weeks or months to do. You should allow for this potential extra time needed when negotiating the option period from the outset. You definitely don't want to be in the position of you option period expiring when you have spent a significant amount of time and money refurbishing the property and making it worth a lot more but now the owner can legally pull out or want to re-negotiate the deal! Once you have the DIP as well as the RICS valuation report these are now very valuable documents you possess for several reasons. You can use them to raise the finance necessary to exercise your option to buy the property.

Let's say you have the right to buy the property for £400,000 and you intend to spend £200,000 to refurbish and create the extra studios. Because you have refurbished the property and significantly increased turnover and profit it now values at £1 million, as per the RICS valuation report. It will now be relatively easy to raise the £400,000 required to fund the purchase. This money can be borrowed on a short-term loan from a private investor, or investors know as 'angel investors' because you can show them the RICS valuation report that shows it is valued at one million.

You explain to the angel investor that the exit strategy for giving them the money back with interest is the bank loan that will raise circa £700,000 on the property (70% LTV). You can also show the DIP to further reassure the angel that it is a relatively safe investment they are making. You will only need the money for a short period of time because as soon as you complete on the purchase you should go straight to loan application with the bank who already gave you the DIP and already have the valuation report to support the loan.

Even though you have already overcome the main significant time delay hurdles you should still be prepared for the bank to be slow in handling the full loan application to get the money into your account, which has taken up to six weeks for me in the past. The reason you need to allow for this is the fact that you will be paying interest on the angel investor's money for this duration which may be at a high rate depending on what you negotiate. Costs such as these also need to be entered into the deal analyser especially if you hope to get all of your money out of the deal with bank finance.

However, based on £700,000 going into your bank account there should be more than enough money to pay the investors back all their money plus interest. If you borrowed the £200,000 to do the refurbishment you should be able to pay those funds back plus interest too. Ultimately you will be left with £300,000 worth of equity in the property, based on the current trading figures, and a high cash flowing business. All this can be done using none of your own money so effectively a hotel for nothing! All that was needed was the right knowledge and education.

I need to make the point here that I didn't wake up one morning knowing how to do property deals like this. I have combined years of experience of different property strategies with going on property education courses. I repeat, people often say that property investment training is expensive, but I know that ignorance is expensive.

Ray McLennan – Dalkeith Aparthotel

“ The County Hotel in Dalkeith, Edinburgh South, had traded as a hotel for over 100 years.

It was a three storey building of 14,000 sq ft with 36 Bedrooms and a function suite accommodating some 300 people. The ground floor had a large public bar area, a reception area and a 50 cover restaurant where hotel guests would be served breakfast and dinner.

It had been put on the market in October 2015 for £899,950 and a year later it still had not sold. The reasons for this were that it required substantial renovation as it had not been upgraded since the late 80s early 90s and was a bit 'tired'. The marketing agents were trying to sell it as a hotel in the traditional sense of the word.

Having had the benefit of attending property courses, and in particular learning about Serviced Accommodation (SA), I had a bit of experience of SA in the Edinburgh market and in particular, identifying what would and would not work. Our original plan with SA had been to purchase specific top floor tenement apartments in central Edinburgh and create additional rooms in the attic space, then rent out the now 4 or 5 bedroom apartments as SA or even as a House in Multiple Occupation (HMO). In addition, we would future-proof the apartments by adding in pre-wired, top of the range smoke detectors and fire sprinklers. Edinburgh is a great University city and a huge tourist destination, especially during the summer and even more so with the Edinburgh International Festival, held every August when accommodation prices spike to double or even treble normal rates. These could be purchased for £180k to £220k - renovated for £80k and would have an immediate capital value of c£350k but could generate a 10% to 12% yield plus a capital growth. Renting as a Buy-to-Let (BTL) could only generate a 5% yield, so this was a better option. The plan was to create 10 of these top floor SA apartments across Edinburgh where demand was second only to London for accommodation. However, two major changes in legislation were on the horizon. On a national level there was Section 24 and on a local level, a total change in how Edinburgh council would approach SA.

One of my contractors had a brother in the local council and he strongly suggested that I "…had a serious chat with his brother…". I made the call. He informed me that the local council had been inundated with complaints about how SA was operating in Edinburgh and fundamental changes were on the horizon. (One thing you ought to know about how we operate is effectively to provide 5* accommodation for 3* people and to future proof all types of rental property by looking at what legislation might affect how property is rented out and what changes there might be.) The planning department brother suggested that I review my SA plans as all future SA premises would have to have their own front door or only whole tenement buildings could be used as SA. In other words, big changes were on the horizon for SA in Edinburgh.

That led to a serious rethink of the SA Strategy. If we cannot do 10 separate apartments with 4 rooms in each, then we would need to see if we could do one building with 40 rooms.

Instead of starting off with £280k and refinancing, we would now need to consider lease options or a purchase of anywhere from £1m to £2m and (depending on the condition of the building) refurbishment costs of a similar amount. The County Hotel was still for sale, so instead of speaking to the agents, I approached the vendor directly. Over a cup of tea, he told me that he was the owner of the building and he had rented it out to a tenant company that had three rented hotels in its local portfolio. He went on to say that the tenant was behind in rental payments and that potential buyers for the hotel had been put off by the condition of the building and the tardiness of the tenant. Despite their lease ending soon, they had wanted to renew it so any new potential owner could choose to keep the existing tenant or take vacant possession.

I originally proposed a Joint Venture (JV) but the vendor needed money to clear off historic bank loans. We created a financial appraisal for the purchase and conversion. This appraisal was checked out by an independent and a few questions arose.

Number one: Were there any capital allowances to be claimed? The understanding was that there could be significant capital allowances available and they could make a significant difference to the overall financial performance of the contract. (Capital allowances can only be claimed once in a buildings lifetime).

Number two: If we do a "What If" on the ratios, what will it look like if there's a delay in the conversion time and additional costs? Delays in larger construction projects can be particularly costly if they are not anticipated or accounted for. Building in contingency costs can alleviate any upsets.

Number Three: SAs are measured in occupancy levels. The local occupancy level was 73%. What if it was only 50% or even 40%? Would the project still be viable?

Once all of these contingencies had been covered, it was clear that this project could only work if a lower purchase price was accepted. I proposed a quick sale and offered the vendor £550k in an email. It was quickly rejected. I decided to call the vendor and talk directly to him but this time explaining the financial appraisal in detail. The vendor considered it but again rejected it. We shook hands and parted on good terms.

Four months later the vendor called me up and asked if the offer was still on the table. I asked if the property was still in the same condition and he confirmed that it was, so we potentially had a deal. To cut to the chase, the purchase price was £550k plus Stamp Duty and legal costs and development finance of £1.1m was secured from Aldermore bank. The redevelopment took 7 months and 33 SA units were created over three floors sleeping 65+ people. The ground floor was rented out as a restaurant, bar and café on a 20 year lease at £40K pa. The tenant spent over £200k improving the ground floor premises. The RICS Valuation showed a GDV of £3.2m.

The first major SA booking for our new Aparthotel came in from a contractor firm for 60 people for 29 nights at £87k! Because they could only book for 29 nights in the system, they contacted us directly and hinted that they had a 6 month contract to fulfil. The occupancy in the first 6 months would be 90% whilst the financial plan showed break–even at 48%. Kevin's CA Surveyor produced a claim in the region of £700,000 which means we won't be paying tax on our profits for at least 3 years!"

I would like to thank Kevin for all his advice and help before and during this project to help bring it to fruition. 𝟗𝟗

#23. Commercial Conversion into SA

Commercial conversions into residential property is a great strategy because there are more and more empty and unwanted commercial properties such as offices and shops available to buy. A couple of reasons for this is a significant rise in people working from home, therefore there is no need to spend time in an office to get their work done, and because of e-commerce there is less need to go to the shops to buy stuff either!

At the time of writing in the UK 'Permitted Development' is allowing these shops and offices to be converted into residential property without the need for planning permission. There are lots of these empty properties available in our towns and cities and the law of supply and demand (in this case over supply) dictates that these properties are relatively cheap. At the same time the price of residential property remains high, which means that residential property (in this case under supply) will remain high and continue to rise.

As commercial conversion is a longer-term strategy than most, this is a reassuring situation. The exit strategy for most developers is to create apartments and sell them on either 'off plan' or when completed, to realise all the equity created from the project. The reason most create apartments is because it's the most efficient way to maximise the number of units created, whilst utilising the existing structure, and therefore maximising the profit.

Prior to selling, the developer will create a long-term lease for each apartment, typically 125 years, although it can be anywhere up to 999 years, for each unit and it is the lease that is sold. The developer who is also the freeholder (unless the freehold is also sold) will usually hand the property over to a block management company, who will take care of things like ongoing maintenance, upkeep of the building and ensure the building is compliant with health and safety regulations. Some developers will own their own block management company to do this.

The leaseholder of each apartment will pay the freeholder, via the block management company, an annual fee to pay for the block management services. The building insurance is usually included in this fee which generally covers the roof, communal areas and the outer fabric of the building. The annual fee is usually paid in monthly instalments. Each leaseholder would need to have their own insurance policy to cover their own liability and everything contained inside their own apartment. The terms of the lease will normally dictate that the freeholder can increase the management fee annually, at least in line with inflation and also to cover fluctuating costs such as insurance of the building. The amount of increase possible varies significantly and so it's definitely worth checking if you are a buyer of a lease!

Instead of selling, some developers will 'hold on' to the apartments and remain as the freeholder and leaseholder. This allows them to benefit from ongoing income from rent and long-term market appreciation of the apartments value. Instead of renting the apartments out on ASTs, an alternative for the developer is to use the properties as SA instead. If the demand is there for SA, this could represent a lot more income for the developer as well as benefiting from market appreciation.

The leases need to be written stating that short term letting is permitted, or words to that effect. The developer must instruct the legal team specifically to write the leases in this way as the default lease wording may prevent the use the properties for short term lettings. If it turns out that SA doesn't work or the market changes, the developer/owner can always revert to renting the apartments on ASTs instead. If you are a developer and considering doing this, something that you should factor in is that you will not be affected by Section 24 whilst doing SA. If the property is owned via a Ltd Co. this is not an issue but if it is owned in any of the other owning entities covered previously, it could make a significant difference to the tax liability.

In my opinion the main reason a developer might choose to hold on to an apartment and use as SA is CAs, if they fully understood the potential size of a claim. If the developer is doing SA with the building, they will be able to claim CAs on the whole gross development cost of the development and any CAs (plant and machinery) acquired that existed in the building, not claimed by the previous owner, that are retained post refurbishment. Again, it is vitally important to claim those CAs before exchange. Even without any acquired CAs, the claim is likely to be significant and could easily run into the hundreds of thousands or even millions, depending on the size of the project.

As with any CA claim the amount often depends on who is doing the claim and so I strongly advise that you use a surveyor who is recommended by someone who has 'kissed a few frogs' in this area!

For example, let's say the CA claim awarded is £500,000. This means the developer will be able to earn £500,000 tax free, and under the sideways relief rules that apply to commercial conversion CAs, they can offset those CAs against other income streams which will significantly reduce their net tax liability.

You may be reading this and thinking that you are unlikely to ever embark on a commercial conversion to SA project any time soon, and if that is the case, it doesn't mean that you can't take advantage of the benefit of doing so for the developer. The way you do that is to take the apartments from the developer and manage them as SA. Most developers will not be interested or simply know where to start in order to run SA and that's where you come in. As previously stated, I always advise that people get familiar with operating SA on their own property or R2SA first, before venturing into managing other people's property, but once you know what you are doing there's no reason why you shouldn't move into management.

The art of successful property investing is creating a win-win situation and managing a developers SA definitely constitutes one of those. By taking the apartments under management you do not have to pay rent for them, nor must you furnish them as you would with R2SA. Clearly you would not need to buy them as they will remain owned by the developer, therefore your initial investment will be very small, and you simply need to plug these apartments in to your existing SA business. You will operate them and once you have taken out your management fees and other costs, hand over the remaining money from the bookings to the owner. Providing the demand is there, the owner could easily earn more than they could from regular tenants on ASTs and not pay tax on £500,000 worth of income!

One of the things my CA surveyor will do is speak to a developer to do a fact find, and then provide an illustration and estimate of how much the CA claim would be if they were to use the property as SA. Do you think if they were told that the CA claim could be £500,000 if they were to hand the property over to you to use as SA it would get their attention? As a professional courtesy to you and to me, my CA surveyor would not allow the developer to cut you out of the deal if it were suggested to him, unless it was proven to him that you were not upholding your end of the agreement with the developer.

Ian Morton –
The Heritage Collection

" I have been in the property business for over 40 years and I consider myself to be a specialist in commercial conversion and since attending the SA course, to broaden my knowledge, I specialise in conversions into SA but I fully intend to go on the training again with Kevin to learn what's new!

I have developed many commercial conversions over many years, and I realised my specialism was the conversion of Heritage property into luxury apartments and houses. I formed "The Heritage Collection" which brings a unique USP to our SA. We built the portfolio, using the buy, develop, refinance and hold model.

I converted a grade 2 Listed Georgian Merchants House in Leeds into a Boutique Aparthotel called "Claremont". This has been amazingly successful and averages over a year £28K per month gross, with around £13K a month net, pre-tax. I wanted to create something new, a hybrid between a hotel and SA using my commercial Interior Designer background and with my interest in history, I wanted to blend Heritage buildings with Contemporary Luxury Living.

I am now developing a whole listed Country House estate in The Yorkshire Dales National Park, called "Marske Country Hall Estate and Wedding Venue". This consists of the Conversion of a group of Georgian Listed buildings. The Main Hall becomes 20 apartments with a Gym and sauna and hot tub with Cellar bars and Marquees on the lawn for large summer weddings. On the 25 Acre estate we are also converting an Old Mill and Garden Rooms into two 12 month a year wedding and corporate event venues. I am also converting the Georgian Stable block with huge equestrian heritage into 10 x 2 and 3-bedroom luxury apartments. I am also looking to expand the estate into luxury mobile homes and luxury Glamping, and I have a major franchise distribution in the UK from an eastern European supplier. This together with wedding venues is my focus, always to build a legacy for my family and future generations.

#24. Development to SA

By Development I mean either building from the ground up or taking buildings that are not currently residential or commercial and converting them into SA. These can be disused property such as outbuildings and barns. Gaining planning permission can be difficult and the property may need a lot of work, but as with any property deal, if you can secure it at the right price there is lots of money to be made.

Mark and Caroline Winship – Gateway Accommodation Solutions

❝   My wife and I have been investing in property for the past 8 years. In 2017, with a healthy portfolio of HMOs up and running and fully managed in the North West and the Midlands we were looking for a second investment strategy closer to home.

Inspired by friends making a success of serviced accommodation we spent the next few weeks assessing demand and identifying a target market for short stay accommodation in an area close to where we live. Our research seemed to indicate a healthy demand for serviced accommodation with several hotels in the area, a nearby airport, some significant infrastructure developments and two large universities within striking distance. Existing serviced accommodation properties in the area were few and far between but we decided to back our research and start the hunt for suitable properties.

We came across a substantial property on the market for just under 500k. Up to that point we had never spent more than 110k on an investment property. On face-value this looked like a step too far but with initial investigation it soon became very clear why homebuyers or arm-chair investors had been walking away from this property for over 2 years and this motivated us to explore creative solutions. The property comprised a 6-bedroom Grade 2 listed family home, some dated bed and breakfast accommodation, a two-storey workshop and some outbuildings, and all within a brand-new conservation area.

The biggest challenge was working out how to buy the property and how to structure the purchase in a way that would allow us to operate serviced accommodation. With no formal records in place, the planning office at the local council were completely at a loss as to how to designate the planning use class of the property and decided to describe it as a 'mixed-use site'. As a result, residential lending was not an option due to the commercial activity on-site and we also hit a brick wall with commercial lending given the presence of a residential dwelling (no surprise the property had been on the market for so long!).

We worked with a solicitor to come up with a plan to split the title. This would contain the C3 Grade 2 listed family home on one title (which made it possible to achieve a normal residential mortgage) leaving the commercial aspect to the property on the other title. We would then process two simultaneous sale transfers on the day of completion.

Prior to exchange of contracts we engaged an architect and an independent planning consultant to create a scheme and a planning proposal for 6x serviced apartments (4x 1-bedroom and 2x 2-bedroom) with C1 planning use class (the apartments would remain on one title). The application was 'called in' by the local parish council but after making our case in front of a committee of county councillors and no small amount of horse-trading with the conservation officer, planning was granted for "C1 serviced apartments.

Back-to-brick conversion is an understatement of the work required to turn these beautiful but run-down buildings into modern executive serviced apartments. One of the outbuildings still had the original manger used to feed the farm animals! We employed a local build team and project manager (a strategy motivated by their local contacts and links with decision-makers in the local council).

You won't be surprised to learn that we encountered challenges along the way- not least the complete absence of foundations which required a significant amount of underpinning! However, this also provided a unique opportunity to plan for serviced accommodation and the needs of our target market from the ground-up. We were able to plan in detail the layout of each apartment with short-stay guests in mind and the amenities that we would like to provide- e.g. HDMI ports built into the walls and hard-wired internet connection to every apartment to supplement a commercial Wi-Fi connection.

We have invested in our own development and education throughout our property journey and having made a commitment to Serviced Accommodation it was a no-brainer for us to enrol on the Serviced Accommodation Training and Mastermind run by Kevin and Caroline. The education and mentoring we received was instrumental in the success of this project and to us launching 9 profitable SA units within the space of 9 months as Gateway Accommodation Solutions LTD.

During the work on converting these apartments which took approximately 8 months, we took on a R2SA property in the same area to qualify demand based on our research and to set up and test our systems. This proved to be a smart decision as it allowed us to refine our processes and iron out any issues that would otherwise have been compounded by launching 6 units simultaneously!

Between August 2019 (launch) and the middle of December 2019 we have achieved 75% occupancy across all 6 apartments. Our cash flow analysis forecasted profitability at 35% occupancy. Guest reviews have been outstanding. Our principle target market is corporate stays linked to the significant industry in the area. With that in mind we produced some direct marketing material promoting our offer as a comfortable and cost-effective alternative to hotel accommodation. One such direct marketing initiative has recently resulted in a booking worth over 40k. Towards the end of the build we instructed Kevin's Capital Allowances Surveyor who produced a report that identified nearly £160k of CA which will result in a tax saving of over 30k!

This development has been fraught with challenges but ultimately life changing. The 6 apartments alone are currently bringing in over 5.5k per month in net cash flow (we expect this to increase) and we are now working towards the 12-months of SA track-record that will allow us to refinance the property in a way that takes into account SA income and we are confident that this will pay back the majority if not all of the build and finance costs. 🙹🙹

SECTION 5: LOGISTICS

We are now getting into the day to day running of the business, and it's vital we get this right in order to make the most profit and to build a business that is sustainable and manageable, but also scalable.

#25. Unit Preparation

From the point at which you get the keys to your SA, there are several things that may need to be done depending on the property.

Property Specific Insurance

Each property will need to have its own cover in the same way that BTLs have their own cover and your broker will be able to tailor the right product for you.

Gas Safety Certificate

If you have a gas supply in the property you should get a qualified Gas Safe plumber to do an inspection and provide a Gas Safe Certificate on an annual basis. There may be a gas boiler, a gas hob as well as a gas fire and so each of these appliances should be certified as safe. Corporate agents such as *Situ* and *Silver Door* may ask for sight of the certificate before allowing a booking, as some of their clients will insist upon it.

Health and Safety Inspection Including Fire Risk Assessment

You should carry out this inspection of the property prior to accepting guests. There is no specific recognised qualification needed by the person doing the inspection, it simply needs to be done by a 'competent person'. I advise that you contact your local authority and ask for their recognised fire risk assessment form.

Portable Appliance Testing

With SA it is best practice (but not a legal requirement at the time of writing) to have a PAT qualified person test each of the electrical appliances in the property and label each of them with the date of the test. A new appliance purchased in the UK from a registered retailer will not need to be PAT tested (if required) until a year after the purchase. Many people think of small electrical items like toasters, kettles and hairdryers, but this applies equally to larger items such as plug in fridges and freezers.

Painting and Decorating

If the property needs to be decorated, you should take the opportunity whilst it is empty to get the painting done. We prefer to use wipeable paint on walls and we use white or magnolia paint from an established supplier so that we are likely to be able to get more of the same for future touch ups. Many people think that white or magnolia is boring but if you opt for other specific colours it will be harder to do touch ups when required if you can't get hold of the same paint you previously used. Paint can go off and change colour with age, so keeping a supply of a specific colour is also not a guarantee of availability.

We have never had a bad review from a guest who was unhappy because of white or magnolia walls! If you add colour with soft furnishings and artwork the place will look great and will be easier to maintain. It's worth mentioning that all white and magnolia paint is not the same and if you use a different brand you will end up with a patchy finish if you are just looking to cover a few marks and not do a whole wall. When we have painted out a property for the first time, we ask the painters to leave some of the paint in a cupboard because this makes it easier for you or your maintenance person to easily do the odd touch up.

Cleaning (Deep Clean)

You should get a property deep cleaned prior to your first guests arriving even if it is a newly refurbished or built property because there are likely to be lots of areas that need specific attention. This deep clean might take several hours and will be a lot easier if the property is empty. The cleaner is likely to pay particular attention to the cupboards and drawers and will focus on any hard to remove dirt that might need different products not used on a normal clean. Please bear in mind that on a normal clean the property must be put back to show home condition and all the beds have to be changed as well, and there won't be enough time allocated to do a lot of 'deep cleaning' which again is easier to do when the property is empty.

Guest Manual

You should have a folder in the property that contains the instructions that came with the appliances. If you don't have the instructions, you should write them out yourself to make it easier for your guests to operate or use things in the property. This could be something like how to use the cooker or how to alter the heating in the property. Remember you guests will sometimes be from overseas and things that might seem obvious to you will not to others. Writing out the instructions yourself will ensure you definitely know how something works so when a guest calls to say they can't operate something, you will know how to explain it. I suggest that you keep your own copy of these instructions per property so that you can refer to them if a guest calls you which will make it a lot easier, rather than relying on memory.

The guest manual is the perfect opportunity to make recommendations for local beauty spots, taxi numbers, things to do with children, favourite restaurants and travel tips such as bus routes. If you have local attractions, you could provide leaflets and maps to assist people finding their way around. Investing time in your guest manual is investing time into your business as the more guests enjoy their stay, the better the review they will give you.

Josh Guest –
Guest Homes Ltd

 Hi Kevin, how do I start?

Life changing, thanks for everything! What a crazy 15 months it has been, since attending the SA intensive course. Before I attended this course, I had already started SA with 3 units however I learnt the hard way without no knowledge - ignorance cost me in the sum of around £15k in the first year. After the course I decided to rebrand the business to Guest Homes Ltd and start to scale the business as I knew I had the confidence to do this after testing the market for several months previously. In the last 15 months I have now scaled up to 24 units, 12 of which are R2SA, 4 R2SA JVs and 8 managed. Cash flowing between £400 - £1500 gross profit per unit. I am now cash flowing around £10k per month gross profit which has been a great achievement for me as most of my friends have just finished University only turning 22 years old recently! I have now taken on employees to help run the day to day business and created many systems which has enabled the business to run smoothly with less input from myself so I can focus on the business development. I am now looking to continue expanding my management services across the UK. The Two-Day Course was full of life changing knowledge, I took everything I learnt over those 2 days and started to implement it into my business straight away! I'd say to others, ignorance is expensive don't be me and just act now with the 2-day course and implement it, you won't regret it."

Welcome Pack

I recommend that you have a welcome pack for your guests that has tea, coffee, sugar and milk (individual UHT portions) as well as toiletries and toilet paper in the WC/bathrooms. We also provide a fresh cloth, scourer sponge and tea towel for each guest as well as washing up liquid and cleaning products in the kitchen. We tell our guests that this welcome pack is to 'get them started' and they should buy more if needed for themselves, because some guests might think you are providing the same service as a hotel which is well set up for this, where usually everything is replenished each day. This would not be cost effective for most SA operators, mainly because it would require someone to go to the property each day in order to do it.

Kitchen Contents

The kitchen needs to be fully kitted out with everything that people would require to prepare, cook and serve meals. Everything you have in your own kitchen at home should be provided. Make sure there is enough for the number of guests, double up on crockery, cutlery, glasses etc. so guests don't need to wash up between every meal.

Furniture

You might already have suitable furniture to use if you are converting a house that you move out of, or you might be converting a BTL which is already furnished into an SA. In either scenario where you are using existing furniture, I recommend that you only use furniture in your SA that is modern and in good condition. I don't recommend that you use any furniture that you care deeply about because accidents do happen with furniture. It's what insurance, deposits and credit card details are for, so yes it can be fixed or replaced but I wouldn't risk it if anything has sentimental value or is irreplaceable. I would also advise that you provide a decent unstained mattress because some of your guests will check it and if it has 'seen better days' you are risking a bad review which is always worth avoiding if you can. I would also recommend a relatively firm mattress because people are more likely to suffer a bad back from a mattress that is too soft than one that is too firm.

Furniture Packs

There are many companies that hire out furniture packs as well as sell complete packs in a 'done for you' type service. Initially I or a member of my team would personally go out and source all of the items needed in an SA, but that is very time consuming and also frustrating. Now all we do is send the floor plan of a property into a company who sell, or lease SA furniture and they send back options of colour scheme and specification/quality which ultimately comes down to how much you would like to spend. It's hard for me to give clear advice on how much to spend on your furniture and equipment that you should provide like a toaster and kettle, you are looking to strike a balance between aesthetics, function and durability. Suffice to say that you shouldn't choose the cheapest, and you shouldn't choose the most expensive!

With the 'done for you service' the company will then deliver everything to your property and assemble it for you and take all the packaging away. When you compare this to marching here there and everywhere to source each individual item as well as colour matching (which is not my forte), unboxing, assembling and disposing of packaging, then you are unlikely to ever want to do it yourself again! Generally, 'done for you' doesn't even cost more so I'm definitely not going back to 'do it yourself' for our business. You will probably still need to source a few things yourself like a

TV and my advice here (at the time of writing) is that you get a 'smart TV' which has inbuilt 'Freeview' channels. These are relatively cheap and allow your guests to access their own TV subscriptions if they have them as well as get access to regular TV.

You should ensure adequate seating is provided for relaxing and eating based on the number of people you are able to sleep in the property. When considering whether to use single or double beds, you will need to take into account your target market, i.e. who the most likely guest type is going to be, as well as the size of the rooms. If families are your main target customer, you will want to have at least one double bed (or larger if the room allows, but consider the convenience of linen), with twin beds / singles in the other rooms. If tradesmen are your main target customer, you will want to provide single beds as they are not likely to be prepared to share!

Bed Arrangements

Zip and link beds are two single beds that can be joined together to make a double/king. The base is usually connected together with a bar at both ends that pivots across from one side and fastens to the other base, and the mattresses have a zip at the side so they can be connected. The size of the single bed bases can vary and therefore the size of the beds together is likely to be larger than a double so make sure you have enough space in the room. Many zip and link bed bases are three feet across which makes the bed six feet wide when zipped together which is a very large bed. Zip and link beds can seem like a perfect solution for an SA operator in catering for different types of guests, some of whom will want two singles and some of whom will want a double bed.

There are significant factors that need to be considered when using the zip and link solution. You will need to have bedding for a six-foot-wide bed as well as for two single beds. This isn't such an issue for the sheets as they don't take up too much room, but it represents three quilts, one of which is very large that needs to be stored somewhere when not in use. You could get the base versions which contain drawers which can help you store the specific linen for the bed. You will have to ask your guests when they book how they would like the beds to be configured for their upcoming stay and you will then have to store that information and convey it to your cleaners. This is an additional task that the cleaners need to check on before doing the 'turn' and is a variable that could go wrong. Sometimes the message will not be passed to the individual cleaner doing the turn or they will forget, and the beds will not be made up as requested by the guest.

The other issue could be that you don't know at the point of the clean who your next guest is going to be. You may have a four-night window available which is booked at the last minute, so how will you be able to configure the beds for whoever books in that period? If the beds have been previously made up by the cleaner as singles, who is going to go to the property to change it over to a double if the next guest requests it, and is there going to be clean linen left by the cleaner at the property in case of this eventuality? We have used zip and link in the past but due to the issues encountered above decided to just have two single beds in a room or a double based on our expected main guest type. Guests can see what they are booking and if they are a couple and decide to book a room with two single beds in it then they will not complain about it and can push them together.

The Sofa Bed

Most SAs will have a sofa bed in the lounge which will increase the number of guests that can sleep in the property. It's important to choose a sofa bed that is comfortable and if space allows opens up to be the size of a double bed. If space is an issue it might only be a single or three-quarter size sofa bed, and in the case of a three quarter, I advise that you only advertise it as sleeping one person to avoid bad reviews. Some sofa beds only come with a very thin mattress which should be avoided if you don't want to get reviews complaining that it is uncomfortable, and you should also choose a sofa bed that is easy to unfold and is fairly robust.

Storing the bedding for the sofa bed can be an issue and so sometimes we use a box that is kept in the bedroom or nearby which ideally you can keep locked. If you have a flat and two people book, you don't want to encourage a third or fourth person who hasn't paid to sleep on the sofa bed and so if you keep the extra bedding locked away, you will save yourself some money on laundry. If the sofa bed bedding is not kept secure then you may have a guest use it, and fold it neatly away again, and so your next guests will find bedding that is not clean.

Pillow and Mattress Protectors

For increased hygiene and to ensure that your pillows and mattresses last longer you should use protectors that can be washed periodically, and this should be scheduled in. We advise good quality quilted pillow protectors that don't rustle when the guest moves. These are readily available in major supermarket chains.

Storage

In my opinion, storage for your guests is not as important as storage for you and your team. Usually your guests will not be staying for a long period of time and even if they are, it's likely that they will be travelling light with the bulk of their possessions left at home. We always try to utilise or create storage for our team of check-in staff, cleaners and maintenance people and we prevent guests from having access unless permitted. A hallway cupboard is ideal for this purpose. With a lockable cupboard you will be able to keep spares like tea/coffee, milk, toiletries and toilet paper for your cleaners to use to replenish during each turn. The cleaners can also use the cupboard to store cleaning products as well as spare linen and towels. We recommend that you have a combination lock on the door which can be incorporated as part of an internal door handle as this looks a lot better than a padlock. If you don't have the option of a lockable cupboard then I recommend that you have a lockable box, which again I recommend is opened using a combination lock because keys are something that can be lost by a member of the team when they are being passed from person to person.

TV Package

At the time of writing we prefer to buy a Freeview TV that can connect to the internet, which allows our guests to connect to their own subscription channels such as *Netflix*.

Internet

Most SAs will provide free WIFI and I cannot stress enough that you must get this right. You should make sure that there is a good WIFI signal in each of your SA units and please resist the temptation of piggy backing off next door's WIFI, even if you do have permission, because the signal will be weaker, and also you want your guests to be able to reboot the router, which is often necessary if the signal drops. I advise having a mobile WIFI router that connects via the mobile phone network as a backup in case there is a problem with the WIFI that can't be fixed immediately. Sometimes an engineer call-out is necessary to fix WIFI and so if you have guests at the time, you don't really want them to go without WIFI as it could lead to a bad review. Before choosing the mobile network, you should check that the signal of that network is strong inside your property.

Interior Design

You should keep the phrase 'less is more' in mind when you are buying your furniture, fixtures and fittings. You should always consider how easy it will be to clean, which should deter you from making the property too cluttered, which also means there are less things to buy and to get broken! You should go for subtle colours and try to colour match your pictures and soft furnishings. Once you have done your due diligence you will know what type of guest you are likely to attract to your SA and your interior design should cater for that demographic. I recommend getting blackout blinds or curtains for the windows to help guests sleep well through the night, or during the day if they are working nights.

Photography

Now your unit is set up, clean and dressed, it's time to get the best photographs to present in your 'shop window', the OTAs and on your website. I strongly recommend you get a professional photographer to take several pictures of each room as well as pictures of the outside. If your unit is in or near a beauty spot, you may want to include photographs of that as well as the property. Professional photography can cost a few hundred pounds, but you will get that investment back time and again with extra bookings, because when people are searching for a property to stay in, good photos will make a property look brighter, bigger and cleaner.

#26. Marketing

You can have the best SA in the world but if you don't market your property properly you will not make much money!

In generic terms, when creating a marketing strategy, you should identify your short and long term goals, be clear about your target market, understand your competitors and their strengths and weaknesses and identify what makes you different. Your marketing plan can then be created to match the goals. As I mentioned earlier, don't rely solely on the OTAs to get customers.

Online Travel Agents (OTAs)

To begin with, most SA operators get the majority of their bookings from the OTAs, who spend hundreds of millions per year on their marketing. This drives traffic to their sites which is great because we can advertise our properties on their platforms for free. There are dozens of OTAs but the two main ones to use at first are *Booking.com* and *Airbnb* and for most people it is vital that they are on both platforms in order to get enough bookings to be profitable.

Booking.com

Booking.com is by far the largest OTA and whilst most of the bookings made on the platform are for hotel rooms, it is also the case that SA operators get the majority of their bookings from *Booking.com*. There are exceptions where *Airbnb* is more popular than *Booking.com* but they are few and far between.

Booking.com is the most complex and time-consuming OTA in terms of listing your properties. You will need to list each property individually on their platform and there are many menus and selections that need to be made to get the most out of the site. With *Booking.com* you are not able to use free text to describe your property, instead you use tick boxes and menu selections to build a picture. *Booking.com* interpret the selections you make and create what they believe to be the best description. You may need to request changes to the description if the system chooses a strange landmark to specify as 'close to' your accommodation. But *Booking.com* will decide whether or not to accept the change. When setting up a new listing, *Booking.com* will take you through a set up process and you will believe you have answered all the questions and then more will appear! Thankfully, you will be shown a 'percentage complete' so you know when you are at 100%.

A significant difference between *Booking.com* and *Airbnb* is that your listing with *Booking.com* is automatically 'instant book' which means that when someone books, as long as they adhere to your terms and conditions and pay, you have to accept the booking. *Airbnb* differs in that you can choose 'enquiries only', which means you can decide whether to accept the booking or not.

The longest single booking you can get with *Booking.com* is 30 nights. Sometimes you will get a relatively short booking via *Booking.com*, but once your customers have checked in, they can book directly with you for subsequent stays, which can be for longer than 30 days and you will therefore pay no commission fee on the subsequent booking.

At the time of writing, *Booking.com* will default to taking payments on your behalf so depending on how you want your guests to pay, you will need to ask *Booking.com* to remove that option and instead pass the payment card details to you / your channel manager. You will also need to ask *Booking.com* to provide the guest's CVC code as this won't happen automatically unless you request it. There are alternative payment options offered to guests, some of which you can opt in or out of. One such option is the use of Virtual Credit Cards. This is where *Booking.com* will take a payment from the guest's actual payment card and store the funds on a 'virtual' card. *Booking.com* then provide the virtual card details to you the operator and you can charge that card with the amount pre-loaded onto it.

This is attractive to guests as it prevents you from having their actual card details and means you are only able to charge them the agreed amount. The downside for you as an operator is that you have no way to charge for damages or extras without getting the guest to provide alternative payment details.

When you get a booking, as a default you will be charged a 15% commission and if you are taking payment yourself you will be invoiced retrospectively. You can opt to pay a higher rate of up to 18% to get a higher ranking on the website, so that when people go on the site looking for accommodation, they will see the 18% commission properties first. This is a good way to get going and to get your initial bookings and reviews. At the time of writing an SA unit needs to have at least 5 reviews before the reviews left by previous guests and the average review score is displayed to people searching on *Booking.com*. As previously stated, many people will not book without being able to see previous reviews and so it might be worth paying the 18% commission until you get your five reviews before dropping back down to the regular 15%. *Booking.com* offer schemes such as 'Promotions', 'Genius' and 'Preferred' which are ways to get your listing ranked higher. You will have to pay extra commission or give guests discounts to be a part of these schemes, but they should increase your bookings.

If you manage to persuade *Booking.com* that you should be allowed to take your own payments (persist long enough and they will allow it), once they are happy that you are a genuine listing they will 'White list' you, which means that you will be able to take payment from your guests in advance of the check in date and you will be able to list additional properties without going through the process of sending a code by post to the property to confirm your ownership (or control) of the property. They do this initially to prevent fraudsters from listing and taking bookings on a property that isn't actually theirs or doesn't even exist! Until you are whitelisted you will only be 'allowed' to take payment from the guest on the day of arrival at the property. There is nothing to stop you from 'asking' a guest who has made a reservation to make payment prior to check in, but be prepared for the guest who reports to *Booking.com* that you have asked them to pay before check in. *Booking.com* will tell you that it's not allowed until you are Whitelisted.

Booking.com also offer reporting and analytics functionality which allows you to see how you are performing against your competitors and your own history. This is getting better and better and can also be really useful to see the effect that promotions have on your bookings.

Airbnb

At the time of writing *Airbnb* has the second largest share of the SA market after *Booking.com* in the UK, but it is set up specifically for SA hosts and guests. It's quick and easy to set up and you can be live within a few hours. If you go on to the *Airbnb* site, you will primarily see whole houses and apartments available to rent whereas if you go on to *Booking.com* you will primarily see Hotel rooms listed. Most guests who book via *Booking.com* are simply making a business transaction as they would when booking a hotel, but with *Airbnb* there is more of a community feel and it's much more of a person to person relationship between hosts and guests.

Whilst *Booking.com* is set up for instant bookings only, *Airbnb* has an 'enquiries only' feature which means that a host can review a guest's profile first before accepting the booking. The guest's profile is visible and reviews from previous hosts on that guest can be seen. If a host sees a profile with lots of previously happy hosts reporting good things about a guest, it is an easy decision for the host to accept the booking. If there are no previous reviews to see because it is a newly opened account or the guest has genuinely never stayed in an *Airbnb* before, then the host can make a decision whether to accept the booking or not. It's worth bearing in mind however that for people who want to make as much profit as possible from SA 'instant book' will need to be activated and not 'enquiries only'. This is mainly due to the fact that if a person is searching for accommodation, they are likely to want to get it booked there and then, rather than waiting for a host to respond to a request.

At the time of writing *Airbnb* always takes the payment from the guest and the money is paid to the host once the guest has checked in. *Airbnb* has a 'Smart Pricing' option which I would not recommend activating because in my experience it offers the property far too cheaply and whilst you are likely to get bookings, you are unlikely to make much profit.

Airbnb provides a decent level of insurance to cover any damage or theft at the property and it is straightforward enough to make a claim. You just need to provide evidence in the form of pictures and initially *Airbnb* will attempt to get the guest to pay and if unsuccessful they will make the payment to you themselves.

Airbnb awards operators who are performing well with 'Superhost' status and at the time of writing this requires the following criteria to be met:

- The average review score has to be above 4.8 out of 5

- The host must respond to guest enquiries within 24 hours at least 90% of the time

- There must be a minimum of ten stays a year

- Honour every reservation unless there are extenuating circumstances that *Airbnb* accept

A Superhost listing will enjoy increased visibility on the site and receive a higher level of support when calling *Airbnb*. Once the criteria above have been met a Superhost badge will appear automatically on a listing. There are also live events hosted by *Airbnb* that a Superhost will be invited to, featuring industry updates and the future plans for the company.

Google

'*Google* my business' at the time of writing is free and it enables you to list your SA properties so that they will appear on a *Google* Search and on *Google* Maps when people search for accommodation in your area. You can show a link to your website, your business phone number, customer reviews and photos. The directions function enables people to see your location on a map and navigate to you using the *Google* Maps directions tool.

Corporate SA Agents

As well as the OTAs already mentioned, there are companies like Silver Door and Situ who mainly target the business end of the market, although they do also support leisure travellers. These agents will encourage businesses to source accommodation for their travelling employees and clients directly through them. SA operators will list their properties with companies like Silver Door and Situ who will usually call the SA operator to try to place a client.

Listing with the Corporate SA Agents can be very lucrative because bookings can often be very long and remember that longer bookings are great because of no voids and less cleaning and laundry costs. The commission that is usually charged is 15% + VAT and the payments are received in arrears. Longer than 28 day bookings are invoiced once a month.

DIRECT MARKETING

Email

Once a guest has stayed in your property it's a good idea to capture their email address for future marketing. With their permission you can email your marketing list with offers and promotions which helps to keep your SAs in the forefront of their mind so that when they go to book accommodation again, they don't simply go on to the OTAs to book and end up staying somewhere else. Remember that there is nothing wrong with inviting a guest who booked with you via an OTA initially, to book directly with you for subsequent bookings which will eliminate the OTA commission. You can invite customers to call you directly, or direct them to your own website. You should offer a discount from the list price on the OTAs which will create an incentive for them to book with you direct, and provided the discount isn't 15% (the typical OTA commission) you will make more money from the booking.

Word of mouth marketing will always be a great source of bookings and you can even incentivise people financially to do this by offering a referral scheme. The easiest way to track this is by issuing an individual with their own code that is tagged to them, which can be used when booking via your own website, or when someone calls you directly.

Leaflets with a discount code highlighted can be given to your guests to take away with them so that they have a physical reminder of how to book with you directly for future bookings. The same leaflets can be distributed around the local area in places where potential guests might be, like the site office/portacabin of a building site, or business/conference centres.

Social Media Marketing

Social media is a good way to market your business. There will always be smart ways to get exposure for free on social media and you should take advice from an expert in this field who can advise you on the best way to do this at that present moment in time for that particular social media platform. Most social media platforms allow you to pay for exposure and reach for your posts which promote your business. Once more you should take current advice on what will give you the best value for money on the different platforms because the algorithms are constantly being altered by the various platforms in a continuing 'cat and mouse' game to allow a certain amount of free marketing, but not too much for free! At the time of writing, here are a few ways to use social media to market your business.

Facebook provides a great way to market to potential customers and you can even target specific people with 'Ad Campaigns' that are much cheaper than *Google* Ads which is where *Booking.com* and *Airbnb* advertise with their huge marketing budgets. You can create your own '*Facebook* page' which is the platform you should use to build up followers and to promote your business from. Your own website link should be embedded within the page using the 'book now' button so that users are redirected to book directly with you. As well as the book now button when you post on your page you should also have a link to your website visible in the copy.

Twitter allows you to have you own account that you can use for your SA business. You can use Twitter to research and engage with companies who may be moving into your area or have won a contract which will need them to place staff and clients in your town or city and 'follow them'. You should post tweets about you SAs especially when you are launching a new unit. When you post you can use the # hashtag function to link your posts to things that people may be searching, for instance Liverpool Football Club are due to play at your local stadium in Bristol and you post "check out this fully equipped apartment available for short term letting" #liverpool #football #accommodation #hotel #bristol. People who are following or searching these things are likely to find you and if they haven't arranged their accommodation yet, you could get a booking!

LinkedIn is a great businessperson to businessperson social media tool and so you should create a *LinkedIn* page for your SA business. You should research your area to find out who the large companies and organisations are, and which construction companies are coming, or already working on building projects in your area. You should look to find out who in that business has a say in booking short term accommodation for employees and visitors. Once you find out who would be a good person to contact at a company or organisation you can connect with them on *LinkedIn*. A good way to find out who the individual is that you would like to contact is to visit the company's website, or you can simply phone and ask who at the company would handle the booking of accommodation for staff and visitors.

#27. Housekeeping and Cleaning

A successful SA business will rely heavily on their housekeeping and cleaning team and you must get the right people working for you to otherwise your SA business will not run smoothly. As it is vital to get the right team in place from the outset, I have covered this earlier in the book in the Due Diligence and Explore sections.

When we take a booking of longer than a week, we do a weekly clean or 'turn', which involves a clean, but not full clean, because all the guest's belongings are still there but we do change all of the towels and bedding. This is the industry standard on longer bookings and is rarely questioned by your guests. In a hotel people would probably question this and expect it to be done more frequently but in an SA it's normal. We explain this when the guest books for longer than a week and cover what we do on our weekly turns, and so if the guest is happy with this they book and pay, if not they don't then we won't end up with a bad review. If a guest wants the weekly turn to take place more often, we can arrange for this, but we would charge more to reflect the extra cost involved.

#28. Guest Communication/ Reviews

This is such an important part of the business to get right because after all, SA is part of the service industry and the way in which reviews are handled will have a big part to play in a successful operation. Only one in nine guests on average will leave a review and so it can take a long time to get a large number of reviews. When it comes to internet shopping, buyers have more confidence in a seller if they can see many reviews and a high average score and SA works in the same way. At the time of writing on *Booking. com* the average review score is only visible once there are five reviews and so with a new listing it's really important to get five reviews in as soon as possible, because some people will not book a property where they can't see a review score, or at least be more likely to book with someone else who has a good average. We have learnt that people are more likely to leave a review if they are asked in person to do so. This is because if they say yes, then they are more likely to because some people will not want to break their promise to you or a member of your team.

You can incentivise your guests to leave you a review by offering them a good discount voucher on any future bookings. If you have your own website that is linked to your channel manager (covered later in the book) you can save on the OTA commission which is typically 15%. You can set the discount however you like in order to get the important review, hopefully a good one, and how much profit you need to make when you take all your overheads into consideration.

The review from your guests is the feedback you need to know that you are getting things right, or that you are not. You cannot pay too much attention to reviews on their own, but an average review score made up of ten or more reviews will paint a pretty accurate picture. If you are getting positive reviews in certain areas, then of course keep doing the same, but if you are consistently being criticised for something then you should take remedial action as soon as possible. Consistently low marks will lower your average, make repeat bookings from the same guests less likely and deter future bookings from potential customers. This might cause your night rate to decrease in order to secure bookings which will impact on your profit.

The way you answer a review is extremely important! I see many operators answering reviews in an argumentative and retaliatory manner which is not wise. Your mindset when you reply to a review should focus solely on a future guest who might be reading the previous reviews and the responses to them before deciding on whether to book with you. If your response is aggressive or defensive or accusatory it will deter someone from booking because he/she will not want a potential confrontation with you either! You should thank the guest for any positive comments and address the negatives in a professional way.

If the guest has said that something is broken then of course check it and respond by saying thank you for bringing this to our attention, we will get this fixed immediately. If something is not broken and it is simply a case that the guest was not 'doing it right' then maybe you could reply by saying you have checked it and it is working ok, but you will leave better or clearer instructions on how something works from now on. As said previously, if you are offering M&G this can often be avoided because if something like a cooker or heating system is even slightly difficult to operate (remember your guests will often be from abroad where things work differently) then physically being shown how to do something, as well has having written or visual instructions, will be a lot easier for the guest to follow and therefore avoid a critical review which will help you make more money.

If the guest is critical of the cleanliness again reply saying that you will address it with your cleaners. Your cleaners are likely to be a little defensive which is human nature, so handle that carefully. A good thing to do here is to incentivise your cleaners to get consistently high reviews on cleanliness. Most OTAs have a specific section for cleanliness which will allow you to isolate the cleaning scores per property. If you have an agreement in place from the outset that you will bring any negative reviews or feedback from guests to the cleaner's attention, then it will not seem as confrontational on your behalf. You could have a bonus system in place to reward high average cleaning reviews which should result in your cleaners continuously working hard and not get complacent, which again is human nature.

Another benefit to having an M&G person is that they can inspect the property for cleanliness prior to the guest arriving, rectify the situation before the guest arrives. We ask our M&G team to photograph any evidence of poor cleanliness (at the time of writing *WhatsApp* works well for this and remember your team member can be on the WIFI and send the photos for free on a Smartphone) and we pass this on to the cleaners for them to address and respond accordingly.

If a guest leaves a review that is just totally unfair you can try to challenge it with the OTA, but in most cases, you will not be able to get the review removed. It is extremely tempting to retaliate and defend yourself and your business here, but it will not help you in terms of making more money. If you respond negatively as stated above it will just deter future bookings. However, if managed well, one single bad review will become out of character for what will become normal for your property. The review could even stand out as unfair and most people reading the review will discount it anyway, especially if they also see you responding in a professional manner, they are likely to be impressed with your attitude to customer service and you can turn a negative into a positive!

Scotty Hodson –
Corporate Gigs and SA Giggles

❝ Hi, my name is Scotty Hodson. This is my journey from having no time and risky cash-flowing contracts to starting a scalable fun and rewarding SA business. I have always been an entrepreneur and digital business owner until some life events pushed me down a route where I was being paid very well to consult on digital contracts. Don't get me wrong I am very grateful for the income, but I have had to sacrifice a whole lot more; that you just can't put a price on.

Essentially consulting and contracting exchanges time for money and it is not scalable. I had to sacrifice my time away from my gorgeous wife and fabulous kids during the week. Sometimes when I got home, I was so whacked and would either miss the kids' bedtime or not have the oomph to read them a book. Sad times! The day always starts very early (missing family breakfast time) spending hours travelling around the country and then having to play the 'corporate game'. Let's just say that often there is a clash of culture, viewpoint and style in doing things. Often, I would have to conform and curb my input, for self-preservation - which winds me up massively. I need to have fun and express myself to be my true self. I was not happy, and I was living a life which was not designed, and I was sacrificing too much of my values and purpose to continue. The time had come to commit to property investment.

I didn't have the spare time or the capital to learn the property game by myself through trial and error, so it was time to upskill and get educated. I went to a property training event to get an insight into what strategies would work for me and my family... Then it happened... Kevin Poneskis hit the stage delivering the SA gospel and some classic one liners. I was all-in. This was the mechanism to give me my time, fun, freedom and family back.

As well as attending Kevin's SA training, I listened to his podcast whilst walking the dogs and driving to the train station. I started implementing everything 'they' told me to do whilst commuting to 'work'. I was able to squeeze in probably 90 mins a day (whilst juggling normal life too). It was a slow start, but I kept on going. It took me six months and one day to get my first unit live (whilst still conforming at work). I kept on learning, and implementing, adapting and improving. The second unit went live after a couple of months and then the third not long after. We now have over 20 units in the pipeline and other business developments that will replace my income, provide scale and allow me to have breakfast with my kids, have fun, and design my life again. We are really excited about how we are growing and improving our SA business.

I will also be pouring all the skills I have used in my past life to improve the 'lifetime value of our guests'. We plan to use technology and ecommerce to transform the industry and deliver our 'Best Stay Promise'. Part of this promise is to 'gift' luxury spa products from our own brand Millie's Organics, designed to improve sleep and calm the senses. It's through creating a seamless experience across all channels and having customer service on point; paying attention to detail to create thoughtful products, gifts and services that truly make a difference. This mission will be scaled nationally through other SA operators where they will receive affiliate commissions for the lifetime of that guest; not just a night's stay.

I am so grateful to Kevin and Caroline for showing me the way, holding my hand when I needed it, and telling me straight when I was naughty. The integrity and passion they have to help people is genuine and together we will go further.

#29. Meet and Greet (M&G)

Meeting your guests at the property comes at a cost to you in terms of your time if you are doing it yourself, or money if paying someone else to do it. I do find however, that there are several benefits to M&G that make this additional cost worthwhile. At the time of writing we pay £15 per M&G. When the booking comes in, the check in is assigned to the M&G person. On the day of check in, the M&G person contacts the guest to establish their likely arrival time and the guest is asked to call when 30 mins away. The M&G person will aim to be there early enough to check everything is as it should be at the property. If the guest is going to be later than the advertised check in window, we advise that there will be a late check in fee which is between £15 and £25 which is used to compensate the M&G person for working at an unsociable hour.

MEET AND GREET BENEFITS

Guest Experience

I find that people generally prefer to be welcomed at the property by a friendly face, which helps guests settle more quickly once they are reassured and made comfortable.

Reviews

You are more likely to get a good review from a guest if they have met and connected with a person as opposed to a faceless experience. It's easier for people to give a bad review on a property if they have not met a person associated with it.

Instructions

It is priceless to show guests how to use things such as heating controls, ovens, showers and even something like how to operate the blinds in the property. This helps because things are less likely to get broken and you are less likely to get a bad review from a guest who couldn't get the shower or heating working.

Bookings

You can pay a lot for someone to devise a market intelligence report for you, but you could use M&G instead to find out more about the guests for yourself, like if they are going to be in town for a much longer period of time than they had initially booked. Often contractors will only book a place for their first week with the intention of finding longer term accommodation once they are in town. Also, with *Booking.com*, at the time of writing, guests can only book for 30 nights and so they may not have been able to book for their full planned stay.

When speaking to the guest in person you can incentivise them to repeat book or extend their stay with you by booking directly via your website. You can offer a night rate that reflects the fact that you will not have to pay OTA commissions and you will also have no voids during the booking, and less cleaning and laundry costs. In fact you sometimes find out that there are many more contractors on the same job who require accommodation in the coming weeks and if you have other units, you can put a package together to incentivise them to stay with you through a direct booking too.

Local Knowledge

You can tailor your advice to your guests in terms of what's on and where. For instance, if it's a young family you can recommend child friendly places to go and things to do. If it's a group of contractors, they might want to know where there is decent pub grub and a not too expensive pint!

Check the Number of Guests Arriving

With formal M&G you have the opportunity to welcome each guest, but it also doubles as an opportunity to monitor the correct number of guests have arrived.

Problem Guests

You can get a better feel for a guest if you meet them in person, which might make you more vigilant during their stay.

Prostitutes

Unfortunately, if you do SA long enough you are likely to get the odd prostitute booking from time to time (see how to avoid bad guests). Your M&G team will become aware of the signs and be able to flag up if they think a guest needs closely monitoring. If you become aware that you have a prostitute staying, in my experience it isn't something that is difficult to deal with. If you tell them to leave or you will call the police, they are likely to just go as they will not want a confrontation with the police. You do not have to refund them as they have broken your terms and conditions, but it is up to you if you choose to give a partial refund.

Last Minute Checks

It is possible that a clean will be missed and not done by your cleaners due to human or software error. Your M&G person will hopefully see it in good time. If the place isn't too messy and there is time, your team member could get the place ready for your guests if there is spare bedding and towels etc. at the property. If not, the guests could be delayed a short time from entering which isn't ideal but better than the guests arriving on their own to an unclean property. If the team member can't clean it themselves then it might be possible to get the cleaners round at short notice to get it done. The other alternative is to accommodate the guests elsewhere if you have an alternative place to offer.

Cleaning Spot Check

Often the first time you will find out that the cleaning is not up to scratch is when you get a bad review. Your M&G person can prevent this from happening by having a look around before the guests arrive. It might just need a quick wipe over here and there or the cleaner may have forgotten to clean the loo which might cause a complaint. The M&G person can take photos of whatever the cleaning issue is and send them to you for you to address it with the cleaners. It is for this reason we often choose not to use the cleaners to do M&G because they are unlikely to flag to you any deficiencies in their own cleaning.

Keys

You cleaner should be the first person to check that the keys for the next guest are where they should be, but your M&G person will provide a double check. There may be several days between the property being cleaned and the next guest arriving, and during this time one of your team or a trades person may need to use the key and so it's important to ensure it is put back in the right place for the next guest. We usually have two key safe boxes, one for guests and one for team and trades, but sometimes the keys are not put back where they should be.

Identification (ID)

M&G is another line of defence against fraud, as ID can be checked against the person arriving at the property making fraud less likely.

Sign in

If the guests are asked to sign in, you have more proof that they stayed with you in the property. We take a picture of their photo ID on top of the sign in form. This makes it much less likely that a guest will claim that they did not stay and then ask their credit card company to reclaim the money (a charge back), but if they do you can provide this evidence.

Point of Contact

Part of the M&G person's duties can be a point of contact for the guest during their stay. Our M&G team know where to draw the line if calls from guests become excessive, but usually the call will simply be for a reminder of something covered during check in, or it may be to report a fault that can be passed on to the appropriate team member to action.

T&Cs

Guests can be asked to sign paper 'terms and conditions' if not already done electronically. This can happen occasionally when guests have trouble accessing their emails whilst travelling, or they aren't able to use technology.

You can see that there are lots of benefits to doing M&G and if it only secures you one large extra booking in a year, then that would make it worthwhile, especially as your average review score is likely to be higher than if not doing M&G. This will give confidence to a prospective guest and make future bookings more likely.

#30. Guest Access

There are a few different approaches to providing guest access aside from M&G. If it is not **extremely** simple for your guests to gain access, you will need to ensure that your instructions are very clear. Some operators use diagrams and photos with arrows and pointers and some even provide video for this, with the links sent out to guests prior to check in. Remember it might seem easy to you after you have done something once, but you must consider that some guests may have arrived from abroad and they might not be familiar with things like key code entry, or a fob that needs to be held next to a panel for instance. I would suggest a 'trial run' with friends or family to test your entry and exit arrangements before unleashing them on the public.

Key Boxes

You may decide to do all of your guest vetting prior to guest arrival and supply access via a key kept in a key box. Many people install key boxes in the doorway of the property, however this isn't always possible, for example in a block of flats where the management company don't allow key boxes to be affixed to the walls of the building. SA operators get very creative when it comes to location for key boxes, including walls in car parks, bicycle stands secured with a chain, the rear wall of a house and many more. When physical keys are used, it's important to make sure the guest knows where to put the key on departure, whether that be back in the key box or through the letterbox for the cleaners to return to the box when they arrive.

WIFI Coded Entry

Entry to property can be in the form of code entry and the codes themselves can be changed using WIFI. Many operators choose this because it can provide better security as guests are not able to lose or copy a key. Once a guest has paid, he or she can be issued the code required to access the property, but as soon as the guest has checked out, the code can be changed via WIFI. A good way to create a code for the guest is to make it the same as the last four numbers of the mobile phone number they provided you when booking. This hopefully will stop them from forgetting what their entry code is during their stay.

Key fobs are often used in blocks of flats to enter the outer door, the door from the carpark and, if there is one, the barrier to the car park. They are convenient to use as an alternative to keys, but they are more expensive to replace than most keys. In SA it is inevitable that one of your guests will leave with a fob (as they do with keys) and it may take time for it to be posted back if indeed the guest admits that they have it. In most instances you would need to purchase another fob from the block management co. This might not be straightforward or cheap and it could create resistance for you using the property for SA. In most cases there will also be a coded entry system as well as key fob entry. I advise that you only issue the guest with the code for entry to the outer door and whilst they are staying with you, they will have access to the apartment.

Claire Powell & Becca Strelzyn – Switchback Stays

❝ Let's start with the show-stopping news - 3 months after first meeting Kevin we quit our jobs!

We run a growing, challenging and exciting Serviced Accommodation business in Cardiff that we're both very proud of. None of what we've achieving would've been possible without Kevin, Caroline and their team.

Our big life-changing moment was when we decided, on a fairly cynical whim to attend a 'Serviced Accommodation Discovery Day' in Peterborough (of all places!).

At that point we were full-time tennis coaches with aspirations of breaking free from the grind. Whilst we enjoyed coaching, we were on the treadmill, exchanging our time for money and battling to find time to do the things we really wanted to do - spend more time with each other, our friends & family and to travel. The goal was to have a business that we could run from anywhere in the world, that generated income without us actually being there and gave us the cashflow to quit our 'jobs'.

When we went along to the SA Discovery Day, we'd had property as a 'side-hustle' for two years. We'd bought and refurbished 2 houses as simple buy-to-lets. The yield was decent (by BTL standards), but not life-changing, and the process was slow. We'd need a heap more cash (which we didn't have) and at least 10 years with property as a side-hustle if we carried on in the same vein.

The Discovery Day piqued our interest and we decided to find out more at the SA Intensive. After the Intensive we became part of Kevin's SA Mastermind. This brought the content to life and gave us the opportunity to access continued support and guidance unique to us and our journey.

How did we quit our jobs after 3 months? We implemented the processes, systems and strategies we learnt from Kevin and the team of mentors. We continue to work hard; we hold ourselves accountable for our own progress and surround ourselves with like-minded people. Crucially we invest money and time in ourselves, in our training and our development.

Starting and running any business comes with challenges, Serviced Accommodation and property are no different. Some days are messy and overwhelming, lots of days are exciting and exhilarating. It's all part of the process of growing our business and we're enjoying every moment. We wouldn't be where we are today without Kevin.

#31. Guest Vetting

SA operators have different approaches to vetting their guests. There is no right or wrong with this and it can be area dependent. You will need to weigh up the risk of getting a rogue, with the additional admin involved in vetting everyone who books. The depth and scope of your checks should give you confidence that the guest is decent and not planning to misuse your property.

Arrange to have your T&Cs or house rules sent to the guest as soon as they book but also make sure the OTAs have the requirement for the contract to be signed as part of the listing so they can support you if a guest is reluctant to sign. Some guests who have ill intentions will cancel and book elsewhere when they see the contract which is a sensible preventative step for parties and other illegal use of the property. Get a copy of the ID of the person making the reservation and a copy of the credit or debit card used to pay which will help you detect fraud and deter possible charge backs. *Google* the phone number used on the booking to see if any 'dodgy' sites come up, as well as checking their social media sites such as *Facebook* and *LinkedIn* to get a feel for the type of person who is booking your property. Previous host reviews are invaluable on sites like *Airbnb*.

#32. Vital Systems and Tools

Channel Manager

A channel manager is a software platform that acts as a hub that connects and communicates with multiple OTAs. If you are going to have more than one property on more than one OTA, it would be prudent to use a channel manager system, because a good one will prevent you from getting a double booking. One of the key functions of a channel manager is that when a booking is received from an OTA, it will block off the availability for that period of time, on all the other OTAs so that you don't get a double booking.

Imagine the scenario where two sets of guests have paid to stay at your accommodation at the same time? Without a channel manager this is likely to happen if people book your accommodation for the same time period using a different OTA, because you were not quick enough to block off the availability after the first booking. If this happens, *Booking.com* and most other OTAs insist that one set of guests will have to be accommodated elsewhere, at your cost in an establishment that is at the same standard as yours or better. This is clearly stated in the terms and conditions that you sign when listing your SAs with them. If you are unable to accommodate them elsewhere, in the case of *Booking.com*, they will find them suitable accommodation (which may be very expensive) and invoice you for their stay. If this happens repeatedly the OTAs are likely to remove you from their site, which in the case of *Booking.com* and *Airbnb*, will significantly impact the number of bookings you receive.

The other main function of the channel manager is to automate many of the processes once a guest has booked. Communication, sending T&Cs, taking payment, sending directions and access details to name just a few. The channel manager is also where you manage your pricing (some will do a bit of this for you) and managing your availability in one place so you don't have to update multiple sites. Some channel managers also have operations functionality which means you can automatically assign tasks such as check ins and cleans at the touch of a button. Some have built in e-sign functionality, allowing you to issue T&Cs at the time of booking as well as chasing the e-signature automatically until it is complete. The more functionality the channel manager has, the less staff members you will need. There is a vast array of channel managers on the market at varying costs. I recommend you get free demonstrations from as many as possible and make your choice based on the size of SA business you intend to build. You will have to weigh up cost versus functionality, reliability and support.

Payment Providers

You will need a merchant account with one of the payment providers in order to take credit and debit card payments. There are many possibilities but the main ones at the time of writing are *WorldPay*, *Stripe* and *PayPal*. *Booking.com* and *Airbnb* can be set up to take payments on your behalf, but even if you are only with those two OTAs, you will still need to take payment for direct bookings and charge cards for damages and extras, so you will need the payment provider as well. Many channel managers integrate with the various payment providers, enabling seamless end to end processing from booking through to payment.

One of the things merchant account providers can help with is reducing fraudulent card payments, and therefore charge backs. You can set your account to a high level of security which will mean the payment provider will check that the name and address of the customer making the booking matches the name and registered address of the card holder and decline the payment if they don't match.

As operators we need to protect ourselves from fraudulent cards because in the majority of cases the banks will support the consumer who reports a fraudulent payment rather than the merchant who takes the payment. For example, a customer books accommodation with you and uses a credit card or debit card to make payment. They have six months to make a claim that the charge on their card is fraudulent and they didn't make the booking or stay at the property. Unscrupulous people may use this method to get their money back, so the more evidence you have that they did indeed make the booking and stayed at your property, the more likely you are to win the dispute.

Sometimes the card owner is a victim as well, as another example is where an actual fraudster has cloned a card and has used it to pay for accommodation. When the genuine cardholder sees the transaction and reports it to the bank as fraudulent, the money will be withdrawn from your merchant account whilst the dispute process is undertaken. In this instance you have very little chance of getting the money as the genuine account holder had their card cloned and so it wasn't a genuine payment.

The best way to avoid chargebacks in either scenario is to collect sufficient information from the person making the booking as soon as they make it, including a picture of their photographic ID and a picture of both sides of the card they have used to pay. A fraudster is unlikely to be able to provide the matching ID and you can also look for specific red flags for card fraud discussed in the debit/credit card section below. Make sure you collect and hold information securely and in compliance with PCI standards. A great way to do this is to use your channel manager as they are configured to be compliant. *Booking.com* are getting better at helping to defend against chargeback claims by providing operators with details of bookings such as IP address, operating system, date and time etc.

Strong customer authentication is coming soon which will reduce the ability for fraudsters to use cloned or fake cards so keep your eye out for that as it will require some small process changes within your business. If you do suffer with a chargeback claim, gather as much evidence as possible, submit a dispute and then sit back and wait. It can take many weeks for a dispute to be resolved and when the decision is made you will receive an email saying you have won, or you have lost.

Credit/Debit Card Details

Debit cards will usually have a 'sort code' and 'account number' on the front of the card and both debit cards and credit cards should have the long number string running straight across the card. Check for unequal spacing or misalignment of numbers, *MasterCard* and *Visa* have 16 numbers divided into four sets of four but remember *AMEX* does not follow this pattern having 15 numbers in three groups.

At the time of writing *Amex*, *Visa*, *Mastercard* and Discover each start with a different number which is always consistent to that card type. *Amex* starts with 3, *Visa* with 4, *Mastercard* with 5 and Discover with 6. Fraudsters don't always remember to match the card type to the initial digit. Taking copies of the card allows you to prove the Card Verification Code (CVC) or Card Verification Value (CVV) number on the card, which is part of remote or online purchase authentication. The three-digit codes are found on the back of the card for *Mastercard* and *VISA*, but *AMEX* has a four-digit code displayed on the front of the card.

Check the holograms which may be on the front or the back of the card. The *Visa* hologram is a dove and the *Mastercard* hologram is two interlocking spheres. Where there are four digits printed on the card underneath the raised card numbers, they should match.

Call Answering/Call Management Services

Call management can be time consuming and sometimes intrusive. There are varying levels of service you can make use of, starting with purely message taking and or call transfer, right through to full 24 x 7 call management. To begin with, a simple message taking service can be quite cost effective and will provide you with an amount of breathing space to look up the guest name and prepare yourself for the call, giving you a more professional sounding service. When you scale up, a more comprehensive service will make your life much easier.

Task Management

There are a number of task management systems available on the market for free. These can be really helpful in setting and managing tasks for yourself and your team. Choose one that can be used on a smartphone so you can be monitoring and updating tasks on the go.

Bookkeeping/Accounting Packages

Unless you love spreadsheets and number crunching, I recommend you get an accounting package such as *Xero* or *QuickBooks* which are reasonable in price and can be shared with your bookkeeper and accountant for them to pull off your end of year accounts and calculate your VAT when you get to that stage.

Document Storage

You are going to be creating documents such as contracts, property inventories, process documents, guest manuals etc. so I recommend you keep them in one place in a cloud-based storage area such as *Dropbox* or *Google* Drive. The advantage of a cloud based service is that your documents are available anywhere there is a device with an internet connection, documents can be selectively shared, collaborated upon in real time, and if the hardware you are using fails, like your PC, then the document is safely tucked up in the cloud. Best of all, most services are free for around 15GB of data before you need to begin paying.

James Mitchell –
Dawton Properties Cambridge

" I started my business on the 14th of May 2018 ready to start in the world of Service Accommodation. I attended my first viewing that evening after chasing a landlord on Gumtree, it took me the next 2 weeks to finally convince him that it wasn't a scam and how the business was going to work. He finally parted with the keys on the 15th of June (literally saying don't make me regret this!). I gave myself 10 days to fully repaint, furnish the whole 2-bed house! Working literally night and day I managed to get it all done ready for my first guests. I ended up doing this exact same thing again and again until I launched my 5th unit at the end of November. To replace my past salary, I needed 5 units as this would be enough to make me financially free. I then set about creating all my systems and automation to really make it hands off, by December we had 2 virtual assistants taking care of bookings and guests so I could focus on growing the business. Achieving my financial freedom hadn't come soon enough as I found out that my Mum had cancer in January 2019, fortunately it was treatable, and I was able to spend a lot of time with her and didn't have a job to restrict me in anyway...

I continued to grow and reached 35 units including a guest house by October. At this point, we had developed a fully automated SA business which I now spend less than an hour a day working on. I had created a £1m business in 18 Months.

SA has been a great platform for me to expand into other areas of the property, support businesses like our cleaning operation and now setting up The Booking Exchange which is going to be a direct booking platform for the service accommodation industry. Attending the training with Kevin was a massive help to give me the springboard I needed to get my business off the ground, Kevin was the first trainer I experienced when I was deciding if I even wanted to go into property, he was very supportive, excellent at answering any of my questions and inspired me to get stuck in! 🔊

SECTION 6: SCRUTINISE

As with any business it's essential to stay on top of the financials and other key performance indicators (KPIs). Let's say you have five properties and on average the bank balance is going up by £5,000 per month, does that mean the business is healthy and can be left alone? You may think so, but what if three of the properties are making £2,000 profit each, one is breaking even, and one is losing £1,000 per month? There is clearly some management action required to turn the loss-making property around to get the breakeven property into profit. It's really important to analyse the performance of each individual property in order to take the appropriate action as well as measuring overall business results.

The main areas to measure within your SA business are Profit, Costs, Review Scores, Occupancy, Capacity, Marketing Results, and Booking Source. Scrutinising the main areas of your business will help you set KPIs for your business but also your team. If you aren't measuring key aspects of the business, then you can't manage the team or their results. KPIs can also be used to reward high performing staff who meet targets for bonuses, provide job continuity as well as determining training and development requirements of staff who do not meet the required standards.

Profit (Also Track as a KPI)

You should be able to see at a glance how much profit you are making on each property per month. A rule of thumb I use is that profit should be around 40% of revenue. If it falls below 40%, a review of the property performance is required to see how to get the costs down or revenue up.

Costs

You should continually look at your costs and see if there are ways to reduce them. Some costs can be reduced as you scale and are able to negotiate better terms with suppliers. Check commercial energy rates, ask regular clients to pay by bank transfer to reduce card fees, claim small business rates relief where possible, streamline systems and processes to reduce staff costs etc.

Review Scores (Also Track as a KPI)

Keep a close eye on your average review scores for each property. You want to stay above 8.5 on *Booking.com* and above 4.25 on *Airbnb*. If your average review score is dropping, look at the feedback and make whatever changes you need to make to get them back up to where they should be.

Occupancy (Also Track as a KPI)

Your occupancy is a key to your profitability (see also capacity) and you want to be achieving at least 70% on average across the year.

Capacity (Also Track as a KPI)

Capacity in conjunction with occupancy can be critical to your profitability. If you have a property that can sleep six people and you are consistently getting bookings for two people, you are missing out on four people worth of extra person per night rates. If this is happening, you should set your base rate higher to discourage the two person bookings coming in and make it more attractive financially for larger groups.

Marketing Results

If you are spending money of Marketing such as *Facebook* Ads or Leaflet drops, make sure you are able to trace any bookings back to the Marketing funnel. If you can't track profit as a result of Marketing spend you have no idea which campaigns are working, and which are not. Track where the results are good and do more of that. Where spend is not resulting in extra bookings, stop that expenditure and try something else.

Booking Source

Analyse where your bookings are coming from, treat OTAs as a shop window or referral agent where it is your job to convert the guests into direct bookings the next time they book. You can use the savings made on the OTA fees to fund your incentives and develop your profit margin.

Accreditation

As SA becomes more mainstream in the UK, it is likely that more accreditation schemes will become available. Currently the main schemes are via the *Association of Serviced Accommodation Providers*, which is the trade association for UK serviced apartment sector, Visit Britain (and its subsidiaries) and the AA. The process involves paying the relevant fees for membership and having an inspection. You won't be aware of which booking relates to the inspector so your standards will need to be consistent to get a good rating. The grading or rating you achieve is based on the entire guest experience from booking right through to post stay communication.

Whilst at the property, the inspector will be looking at the quality of the accommodation, including the standard of furniture, the decor, soft furnishings, the standard of cleanliness including hard to spot areas such as under beds and tops of doors, the amount of amenities provided based on the number of guests you can accommodate including cutlery, crockery, lamps, pillows etc. Another major aspect of the rating will be based on your attention to Health and Safety including firefighting equipment, risk assessments, first aid kits etc. The accreditation schemes all work differently and have different costs associated with them as well as different minimum numbers of units.

#33. Summary

I hope you have enjoyed this book and can see that Serviced Accommodation in its many forms represents a significant opportunity for someone to cash in on this very exciting strategy. There has never been a better time to get into SA because of the trend towards SA and the significant tax breaks that exist for SA operators and owners.

The DEALS system that I have created provides an end to end process to follow that will enable you to source and manage SA property. The DEA will take you all the way to acquisition. You may choose to go ahead with acquisition yourself or you may opt to source the deal on, and charge a fee, to someone else to operate. If you do intend to operate/manage the property yourself then the LS comes in to play. Once you have mastered the LS yourself you can offer to operate other people's properties for them as SA on a management basis. There are multiple ways you can use the DEALS system depending on your area of expertise and your personal circumstances. Examples of this are:

Deal Sourcing

Once you can do and fully understand the DEA of DEALS you could decide to source or package the deal on instead of taking it for yourself. The investor would give you a sourcing fee and take the deal for themselves. This could be an SA deal for some to buy or rent. Packaging on R2SA deals is a much quicker way to earn packaging fees because there is no need to wait for exchange or completion for the packaging fee to be paid.

Full Management

With the LS of DEALS, once you have all of your systems and team in place to manage your own properties you could offer the same service to others and charge a percentage of revenue for doing so.

Cloud Based Management

You could simply plug someone into your online systems such as your website, channel manager and merchant account and charge a smaller fee for this service.

Photography

You could provide this service to other SA operators if it is a passion of yours and you have perfected the photos of your own units. You will know exactly what is important for an SA operator when it comes to the photos and how best to show off the benefits of an SA to prospective guests to make it more likely for them to book.

Property Staging

If you have a flair for this, it is definitely a service that you can offer to others. Your own website and listings can be your own advert to showcase your skills. Many people, including me, do not have an eye for interior design therefore these skills can be marketed. It can be a labour intensive task furnishing and equipping an SA unit and well worth paying for. A combination of the two services would be a great 'one stop shop' for someone with limited time or skills. I often hear people do this for themselves for their first unit but declare that they will definitely outsource it next time!

Cleaning

You could scale out your own cleaning company to service other SAs in the town because you will know how to tailor your service to make it more appealing to other operators.

Laundry

I have trained people on my SA course who already had a laundry business, but they wanted to have a better understanding of how SA operators think and work so they could better tailor their service for the growing SA market. Your own laundry business could be an option especially if you scale your own business significantly.

Meet and Greet

Once you have trained up your own M&G people you could offer this service to other operators who may be too busy to do it and don't have their own people to rely on.

Facilities Management

Repairs that need to be done at short notice in an SA property can be difficult to manage and so offering this service to others would work well.

Listing Optimisation

One of the things I teach on my training is how to make a listing on a website or on an OTA stand out to make it more likely to get bookings. The photos have to be good but also the order in which they appear is fundamental when it comes to making a prospective customer book your property. A good way to do this is to get the opinion of a group and ask them to tell you which photos in order of preference would make them stop scrolling and book your place. You will now know which photos to front load on your listing to grab people's attention. The wording on sites like *Airbnb* needs to be good to showcase the property and what it has to offer. If you have a skill for doing this, you could offer this service. This is something you could do from home online. If your business is in one town you could offer the service to SA operators in other towns so that you do not increase your own competition! To find the listings that are in dire need of your services you could simply go on the OTAs and the evidence will be there for all to see. This service could be linked with property staging and photography because at the end of the day, a phrase I remember from my army days was, there is no point in trying to polish a turd!

I hope this book has given you the belief that you can create significant income from property so that you can create the life changing recurring income you need to take control of your financial future. Most people spend their lives exchanging time for money, working hard to make someone else wealthy (in the private sector) in a J.O.B. But what if you no longer need to rely on a job anymore, or the business that you are currently in, which might not be giving you what you want from life. It could even be that you have already retired but you want to create more income to enjoy a better retirement! Or you might be in school or university and not want to enter the job market but would prefer to become a property entrepreneur instead. Whatever your circumstances, I hope this book gives you hope and excitement for the future. I will never say that Serviced Accommodation is easy because no property investing is. It requires hard work and determination to succeed, but I will say that it is the best hard work you will ever do in terms of providing financial security and a legacy for yourself and your family. My experience tells me that people are many times more likely to become successful as a property investor if they also attend a good reputable training course. You can visit my website www.propertysoldier.co.uk for more information on the training courses that I provide.

Here's to your ... **Serviced Accommodation Success!**

Glossary of Terms

AST - Assured Shorthold Tenancy	LTV - Loan to Value
B&B – Bed and Breakfast	M&G - Meet & Greet
BNI - Business Network International	OPM - Other People's Money
BTL - Buy To Let	OTA - Online Travel Agent
CA - Capital Allowance	PA - Personal Assistant
CT - Corporation Tax	PCI - Payment Card Industry
DIP - Decision in Principle	R2SA - Rent 2 Serviced Accommodation
EBITDA - Earnings Before Interest, Tax, Depreciation and Amortization	RVU - Rateable Value per Unit
FHL - Furnished Holiday Let	S24 - Section 24
GDPR - General Data Protection Regulation	SA - Serviced Accommodation
GDV - Gross Development Value	SBRR - Small Business Rates Relief
HMO - House in Multiple Occupation	SBS - Single Bed Space
HMRC - Her Majesty's Revenue & Customs	SSAS - Small Self Administered Scheme
ICO - Information Commissioner's Office	SIPP - Self Invested Personal Pension
IFA - Independent Financial Advisor	ST - Sole Trader
IO - Interest Only	T&C - Terms & Conditions
JV - Joint Venture	TOMS - Tour Operators Margin Scheme
LA - Letting Agent	UBR - Uniform Business Rate
LLP - Limited Liability Partnership	VA - Virtual Assistant
LO - Lease Option	VAT - Value Added Tax
Ltd Co. - Limited Company	VOA - Valuation Office Agency